Praise for

Eleanor in the Village

"The story of [Roosevelt's] liberation . . . a complete portrait of a pioneering feminist and pivotal political figure."

—*New York Daily News*

"[*Eleanor in the Village*] fills in some vital history that adds to Roosevelt's legendary life. . . . Triumphant short chapters of her time abroad and her time in the Village ('The Making of a Heroine') are both moving and beautifully observed. As is the account of Eleanor's devotion to Franklin during his physical recovery and political resurrection, becoming the Democratic nominee for president after his debilitating illness made the prospect seem unattainable."

—*New York Journal of Books*

ALSO BY JAN JARBOE RUSSELL

The Train to Crystal City:
FDR's Secret Prisoner Exchange Program and America's Only
Family Internment Camp During World War II

Lady Bird: A Biography of Mrs. Johnson

They Lived to Tell the Tale (editor)

A view of iconic Washington Square Park in Greenwich Village

Eleanor in the Village

Eleanor Roosevelt's Search for
Freedom and Identity in
New York's Greenwich Village

JAN JARBOE RUSSELL

SCRIBNER

New York London Toronto Sydney New Delhi

PHOTO CREDITS *frontispiece:* Browning Photograph Collection, PR 009, New-York
Historical Society, 60727; *photo insert:* (1) Eleanor Roosevelt, Public Domain, via Wiki-
media Commons; (2–4) Franklin D. Roosevelt Presidential Library & Museum; (5)
Lucy Page Mercer, Public Domain, via Wikimedia Commons; (6) Billy Rose Theatre
Division, The New York Public Library; (7–8) Yale Collection of American Literature,
Beinecke Rare Book and Manuscript Library; (9) Unknown author, Public Domain,
via Wikimedia Commons; (10) Library of Congress Prints and Photographs Division,
LC-DIG-npcc-25287; (11) Courtesy Municipal Archives, City of New York; (12–14)
Franklin D. Roosevelt Presidential Library & Museum; (15) Hennepin County [Minn.]
Library; (16–17) Franklin D. Roosevelt Presidential Library & Museum; (18) Library of
Congress Prints and Photographs Division, LC-DIG-ppmsca-70147; (19) Franklin D.
Roosevelt Presidential Library & Museum; (20) National Archives (195433).

This book is in memory of my mother, Laverne Jarboe, a gifted schoolteacher, who was proud of Eleanor Roosevelt. Like Mrs. Roosevelt, my mother had a great mind as well as creative energy. Eleanor served as a role model for my mother, as she did for so many women. My mother's three sisters, LaNece, Sharon, and Diane, also admired Eleanor's life.

Despite all criticism, she "had the courage to be herself
and to do the things which seems right to her."
As one Gloucester fisherman was heard to say:
"She ain't dressed up, and she ain't scared to talk!"
—*Blanche Wiesen Cook,* Eleanor Roosevelt,
Volume I: The Early Years, 1884–1933

Contents

CONTENTS

Eleanor in the Village

The Gilded Age in New York City

The Vanderbilt grand costume ball, planned for Monday, March 26, 1883, was Manhattan's most anticipated party of the year. The gala was to be thrown by Alva Vanderbilt, the wife of William Kissam Vanderbilt, known as Willie, who had been fortunate enough to be born the grandson of the railroad baron Cornelius Vanderbilt. Willie, about six feet tall, with dark hair carefully parted down the middle of his head, was well known for managing his family's railroad investments; as a man of wealth he also bred horses and later enjoyed "motor racing."

Willie and Alva were determined to make their mark in New York society. Alva had attended boarding school in France and had a passion for all things French—the language, architecture, tapestries, clothes, and jewelry. She wanted her home to resemble the largest, most chic mansions in France, and her costume ball to be a spectacle of excess that would amaze and impress the lucky twelve hundred colleagues and friends of the Vanderbilts who would receive invitations. Any New Yorker who was wealthy waited desperately in hopes of witnessing the lavish affair Alva would create.

At that moment in the Gilded Age, New York was known for the behaviors, customs, and density of its wealthiest citizens, most of whom preferred to live among similarly affluent folks. Indeed, many well-heeled New Yorkers had moved away from Manhattan's waterlines along the Hudson and East Rivers, away from the busy docks and shipyards, which had become rough and dangerous. Alva Vanderbilt and the other wealthy women in New York were dogged about impressing upon others that their families were rich and therefore important. The greatest wealth of the city was now found in the townhouses, apartment buildings, and hotels concentrated within a wide swath of city blocks in the center of the island, running from Bowling Green Park at the southern end to Washington Square Park in the Village, then on up to Madison Park, and from there to Central Park and 57th Street, which glimmered in Thomas Edison's newly invented streetlights.

Meanwhile, on the Lower East Side, neighborhoods of poor immigrants—Jews, Italian, Germans, and Chinese— lived packed in small apartments that often housed multiple extended family members. Families even rented out rooms to make ends meet. The immigrants brought their own cultures with them to New York and would in time form new communities intermingled in the melting pot. Many of the working class gathered on the Bowery after work, where a dime could buy distraction in a bar or some other convivial venue. The Age may have been Gilded, but a great disparity endured between the few rich and the many, many desperately poor.

Yet even Alva Vanderbilt, as wealthy as she was, had her share of what she might consider a struggle to move up in the world. When Mrs. Vanderbilt decided to throw a ball at her home, she took direct aim at the older Mrs. Caroline Astor, who then dominated the social scene in New York. Mrs. Astor and her social secretary, Ward McAllister, had in earlier years created a list of four hundred of the wealthiest people in New York, called "The Four Hundred," the only ones acceptable in fashionable society. On Mrs. Astor's list were prominent businessmen, politicians, society matrons, people who were born with fortunes—unlike the Vanderbilts, who had earned their wealth with the railroads, and were thus considered nouveau riche and therefore inappropriate guests for any celebration of Mrs. Astor's.

The Astors' massive fortune derived from generations of Astors, including William Backhouse Astor Sr., and was passed down and expanded by his two sons, John Jacob Astor III and William Backhouse Astor Jr., Caroline Astor's husband. Their estimated net worth was well over $100 billion in 2019 dollars. Even so, William Backhouse Astor Sr. regretted the bargains he had missed in real estate. When a reporter asked him why, the senior Mr. Astor said, "Could I begin life again, knowing what I now know, and had the money to invest, I would buy every foot of land on the Island of Manhattan." Given the Astor fortune and the fact that the Vanderbilts were not on the list of the privileged four hundred, Mrs. Astor felt that Alva and Willie's costume ball was well beneath her and had no interest in attending.

Her daughter Carrie felt differently, though. She begged to attend the party, because she didn't want to be left out from her friends. There was a problem, however—Mrs. Astor had not received an invitation, because she and her daughter had never properly "called on" Mrs. Vanderbilt, which amounted to a major faux pas in the upper echelons of Gilded Age society. Now, despite Mrs. Astor's view that Mrs. Vanderbilt was made of "new money," Mrs. Astor recognized that Mrs. Vanderbilt was a social force to be reckoned with. When Mrs. Astor swallowed her pride and dropped her visiting card at Mrs. Vanderbilt's home, she received an invitation to the ball the next day.

As the gala drew closer on the calendar, Alva Vanderbilt stirred up excitement by giving a few journalists a sneak preview of what would soon delight her guests. She escorted the newspapermen into the mansion through a large marble door, to see a dazzling world . . . lovely Japanese lanterns were strung from beautiful columns and the third-floor gymnasium had been converted into a forest filled with palm trees, bougainvillea, and orchids. The newspaper descriptions would soon fill the most fashionable citizens of the city with anticipation.

Finally, on the evening of March 26, 1883, carriages arrived at the mansion at ten o'clock, earlier than Alva

Vanderbilt had expected. Uninvited onlookers surrounded her home and strained to get glimpses of the lovely debutantes with their pearls and gloves and any and all other society loyalists, tonight dressed as pirates, ghosts, animals, gypsies, and others. Meticulous research had gone into the costumes, and *The New York Times* expected men to be there dressed as "Cardinal Richelieu, Otho the Barbarian, or the Count of Monte Cristo, while the ladies have been driven to the verge of distraction in the effort to settle the comparative advantages of ancient, medieval, and modern costumes." New York police, armed with batons, cordoned off the entrance but still had their hands full keeping those who didn't belong under control.

Meanwhile, early arrivals were welcomed between ten o'clock and eleven thirty, and New York's most fashionable women were shown into the house and escorted to grand bedrooms bedecked with tapestries on the walls and mirrors on the ceilings. Their maids stayed behind in carriages and were summoned as needed. Every surface was worthy of ogling and admiration: walls painted with lovely apple blossoms, bathtubs carved of alabaster. In one room, a silent woman dressed as a nun in black robes sat writing at a table. She had been placed at the table as a prop, a fanciful oddity, someone for the wealthy women to watch as they awaited one another's entrance.

At eleven thirty that evening, Alva Vanderbilt descended the grand staircase dressed as a Venetian princess, complete with a Venetian cap covered with magnificent jewels. She held two white birds in her hands. Willie appeared as the "Duc de Guise," meaning the Duke from the House of Guise, a noble French family; he was adorned in yellow silk tights, a short yellow jacket, and a black velvet cloak embroidered in gold. Husband and wife led the first dance of the evening as the others joined them in the fantasy world dancing to life around the grand staircase.

All of the women were intrepid in their choice of costumes. Alva's sister-in-law, Alice Vanderbilt, inspired by Edison, came dressed as "The Electric Light" and carried around the dance floor an illuminated torch powered by batteries buried deep in her gown. Miss Edith Fish dressed as the Duchess of Burgundy, with sapphires and rubies sewn into the front of her dress. Kate Fearing, known as "Puss," commissioned a gown meant to honor her pets, with a stuffed cat set upon her head and seven cat tails sewn into her skirt. The women had opened their private vaults for the night; they swirled and swished festooned with sapphires, rubies, pearls, and most importantly—diamonds. Wives literally dripped with diamonds, displaying not only their social status but their husbands' wealth.

Somewhere in this extravagant crush stood Anna Hall and Elliott Roosevelt, a young, prominent couple who would be married later that year at Calvary Church, the socially acceptable Episcopal church near Gramercy Park. They were beautiful and heartbreakingly young. Anna had just turned twenty, and Elliott twenty-three. Anna had been well instructed by her parents and maintained flawless manners. "Fair, frail, and fragile, and therefore a good illustration of beauty in American women," wrote one society columnist. Once, while Anna sat for a portrait, the poet Robert Browning was so transfixed by her beauty that he rested on a bench and read to her from his latest collection. Everywhere Anna went, she was the most watched and envied woman in the room. She had dutifully followed all the rules of the Gilded Age: she had launched the Knickerbocker Bowling Club, inaugurated a series of dances, promenaded in Central Park in a carriage driven by her handsome future husband, and cheered him on at his many polo matches, yacht races, and horse shows.

On that night, the sparkling events at the Vanderbilt ball would quite naturally have appeared to Anna and Elliot to be another moment emblematic of untold promise and beauty ahead for the two of them. Little could they have known that what they youthfully believed about their own gilded destinies would in time be destroyed.

CHAPTER 1

New York, New York

I think at a child's birth, if a mother could ask
a fairy godmother to endow it with the most useful gift,
that gift should be curiosity.
—Eleanor Roosevelt

Eleanor was born into an old and large clan of Dutch merchants who had arrived in the seventeenth century and settled in the colony of New Amsterdam at the southern tip of Manhattan. The first of the Roosevelts in New York were Claes Martenzen van Roosevelt and his wife, Jannetje, who arrived by ship from Holland sometime before 1648. Eight generations of Eleanor and Franklin Roosevelt's ancestors built fortunes as importers of West Indian sugar, as bankers, and as speculators in Manhattan real estate. All of the Roosevelts who came along after the seventeenth century were born on Manhattan Island, but in time the clan split into two groups: the Oyster Bay Roosevelts on Long Island, who were associated with Eleanor's father, Elliott, and with her uncle Theodore, and who belonged to the Republican Party; and the Hyde Park Roosevelts, who, by

9

contrast, were linked to James Roosevelt Sr. and Sara Delano Roosevelt, parents of Franklin and supporters of the Democratic Party.

Oddly, both future presidents, Theodore and Franklin, suffered from childhood illnesses, although Franklin's would not afflict him until he was thirty-nine years old. Teddy was three when he came down with severe asthma and was not expected to live. As he grew older, "Teedie," as he was called by his mother, was not permitted to go outside to play or go to school. But when he was twelve, his father began to lecture him on the importance of developing his body to develop his mind, and to accommodate his father, Teddy took to rowing in Oyster Bay, riding horses, and showing off his muscles in other ways. But he also learned the power of words, writing in his journal of sickness: "Life itself was always an ongoing battle."

Prior to Elliott Roosevelt's marriage to Anna in December of 1883, it was assumed that he would become the most successful of the Oyster Bay Roosevelts. He went to work in Manhattan with the leading real-estate agency in New York, the Ludlow Firm, which paid him an annual income of $15,000 ($400,000 today), enough to afford a brownstone in the fashionable 30s in Manhattan. He hoped to make a fortune in real estate and follow Teddy into politics—but Elliott did not possess the passion to help people that energized his brother, who was one year older.

Born and bred New Yorkers, the Roosevelts had watched in the 1830s as the city sprawled north up the island as far as Houston Street. By 1883 the city had its first railroad, the New York and Harlem, which sparked and made a great deal of noise running from a ticket office at Prince Street up the Bowery and what was then called Fourth Avenue, to Sunfish Pond, near the corner of what is now Park Avenue and 32nd Street. Modernity kept arriving with new contraptions and conveniences: in May 1878, American Bell licensed the Metropolitan Telephone and Telegraph Company to commence service in all directions from City Hall. The first subscribers numbered 189 and paid $60 a year (approximately $1,700 in today's currency), which was quickly raised to $150 ($4,200). Meanwhile, on September 4, 1882, Thomas Edison directed current into eight hundred lamps that shed light on two locations—the New York Times Building and the Drexel, Morgan & Co. Building, where Edison watched this heroic event.

The Roosevelt families were well aware of the dramatic growth taking place in what was becoming the largest city in the United States. In 1885, Theodore Roosevelt became a state assemblyman and scoured the slums of New York, where he found that tenement-dwellers worked long hours each day. Cigar-making, for example, was done by the immigrant poor in squalid, crowded rooms.

Here is what Teddy wrote of what he saw: "The work of manufacturing the tobacco went on day and night in the eating, living and sleeping rooms. . . . I have always remembered one room in which two families were living. On my question to who the third adult male was, I was told that he was a boarder. There were several children, three men, and two women in this room. The tobacco was stowed about everywhere, alongside the foul bedding, and in a corner where there were scraps of food. The men, women, and children in this room worked by day and far into the evening, and they slept and ate there."

In May 1895 Teddy Roosevelt became president of the New York City Police Department and brought his strong personality and his philanthropic zeal to the job. He prowled the streets alone at night and often found some of his blue patrolmen sleeping on the job or engaged with prostitutes. With his rasping voice and piercing eyes, Teddy rebuked them and continued to watch to make sure they did their duty. Pedestrians on the street stopped him and thanked him for doing his job. Roosevelt rode his bicycle to the railroad station and then went to work by train. By then, bicycle riding had swept New York, and he initiated the idea of putting a few patrolmen on bikes; when that was a success, even more patrolmen began riding them. In the first year, the bike squad made more than a thousand arrests. In a relatively short time, Teddy's profile and his crusade against corruption in law enforcement made him a household name in New York. He was known for having a heart for the poor as well as easy access to the rich and famous.

Teddy Roosevelt proved to be too much of a working man for his brother, Elliott. Instead of embarking on a career in politics, Elliott became enamored of polo matches, yacht races, horse shows, and liquor. A weakness for alcohol had surfaced early in life. He was prevented from attending a university after an attack of epilepsy that was later diagnosed as a dependence on alcohol. When Elliott was older, he and Teddy took a hunting trip to the "Wild West" of Minnesota and Iowa. Teddy later noted his alarm about his brother's drinking and wrote to their younger sister, Corinne: "As soon as we got here he took some ale to get the dust out of his throat; then a milk punch because he was thirsty; a mint julep because it was hot; a brandy smash . . . and then sherry and bitters to give him an appetite." Teddy blamed Anna, Elliott's wife, for not keeping a firm hand on him and he encouraged Elliott to stop drinking and get to work. "Anna, sweet though she is, is an impossible person to deal with. Her totally frivolous life, as was inevitable, has eaten into her character like acid," Roosevelt wrote.

At first, Anna did not worry about her husband's drinking because most men in their wealthy group of friends were heavy drinkers. She looked forward to summers when Elliott and his elder sister, Bamie, would travel from New York to Meadow Brook, Rhode Island, then up to Bar Harbor, Maine, and back to Newport, Rhode Island. "We play our polo matches on Monday and Saturday; next we go out on Mr. E.T. Gerry's yacht the Electra," wrote Anna. "We dine, dance, play tennis, polo, swim and live in the open air all the time." And Elliott drank.

On a fall day in October 1884, the eleventh, Anna gave birth to her daughter Eleanor at her parents' brownstone at 56 West 37th Street. She delivered Eleanor without complications, but her first words to Elliott afterward were harsh: "She is a little more wrinkled and has a less attractive body than the average baby." Elliott disagreed and thought that baby Eleanor was beautiful; a "miracle from heaven." This disappointment from her mother and adoration from her father at her birth became the opposing mirrors in which Eleanor saw herself. In later life, she believed she was an ugly duckling around everyone but her father, with whom she could be her true self.

Eight months prior to her birth, Eleanor's family had suffered unexpected losses. Martha "Mittie" Bulloch Roosevelt, mother of Bamie, Teddy, Elliott, and Corinne, died of typhoid fever on February 14, 1884. In the same house two days earlier, on February 12, 1884, Alice Roosevelt, Teddy's wife, had given birth to an eight-pound baby girl, Alice. Teddy, then a state legislator in Albany, received a telegram from Elliott telling him that his wife Alice was seriously ill and that he needed to come home. Teddy jumped on a train and reached Manhattan late on Wednesday, February 13. An ashen-faced Elliott met him at the door and said, "There is a curse on this house." Devastated, Teddy went to Alice's bedside. The doctors told him that she was battling what was called Bright's disease, a failure of the kidneys. In the predawn hours of Thursday, February 14, Alice died. "The light has gone out of my life," Teddy wrote in his diary that day below a large black X. He believed that having a large family was one of the highest obligations of a man and often said that children were God's blessing to humanity. The blow to both Teddy and Elliott was enormous. Teddy had lost his mother and his wife on the same day. He fell into a depression and repeated a saying again and again that brought him back to his work: "Get Action. Do Things. Be Sane." To keep himself steady, he gave his daughter to his sister Bamie and left Manhattan to get back to work.

Thus did a cloud loom over Eleanor. Her babyhood was shrouded by death. In the archives of the FDR Library are the typed notes that Joseph Lash, a friend of Eleanor's who wrote a biography of her, based on his interviews with a prominent New York child psychiatrist, Viola Bernard. Dr. Bernard said that in psychological terms, Anna viewed Eleanor's birth "as a death threat. . . . There had been the death of Teddy's wife in childbirth. Anna was disappointed because Eleanor was not a boy—that was the atmosphere in which she was born. Eleanor came into the world guilty and had to reinstate herself."

Eleanor saw herself from a point of disassociation; even as a child she hid herself for fear of being seen. She assumed that she would be rejected. In her *Autobiography*, Eleanor described herself as a "shy, solemn child even at the age of two, and I'm sure that even when I danced I never smiled." She remembered walking down the stairs of the house to the library. "I wore a white frock and stood bashfully, very often with my finger in my mouth, waiting at the door for my mother to call me."

"Come in, Granny," her mother said with exasperation.

And Eleanor wrote: "I wanted to sink through the floor in shame. She often called me Granny, I was without beauty and painfully shy and I seemed like a little old woman lacking in the spontaneous joy and mirth of youth." She was rejected by Anna, who described her child as "old-fashioned" and "ugly" and told her friends she could barely force herself to look at Eleanor. Her mother's lack of affection became the source of Eleanor's original wound—the idea that she was unloved—which never left her.

In contrast, Eleanor's father was gentle and viewed Eleanor as gifted and remarkable. "My father was always devoted to me. . . . As soon as I could talk, I went into his dressing room every morning and chattered to him often shaking my finger at him," Eleanor remembered. "I even danced for him, intoxicated by the pure joy of motion, twisting round and round until he would pick me up and throw me into the air and tell me I made him dizzy."

In *FDR: A Centenary Remembrance*, Joseph Alsop, a famous journalist of the era and cousin to the Roosevelts, wrote that one day when his mother was having tea with her cousin Anna Roosevelt, Anna turned to her daughter and observed: "Eleanor, I hardly know what's to happen to you. You're so plain that you really have nothing to do except to be good." Alsop believed Teddy's theory that behind Anna's beauty was "a rigidly conventional woman who somehow combined religious devotion and intense worldliness." The way Alsop saw it, Eleanor could never please Anna, who "had eaten into her daughter like a cancer."

Photographs of young Eleanor reveal that she had her own unconventional source of beauty. Her long blond hair tumbled down her shoulders, her hands carefully folded on her lap or nestled in a cummerbund at her waist, and her grave blue eyes avoided the camera; her pale smile appears plastered on her face, and her mouth is shut as if she were afraid to speak. Her mother criticized Eleanor severely for sucking her thumb, a habit that pediatricians later ascribed to the child's hunger for soothing. Anna wrote to Elliott's sister and told her: "Baby has grown fatter and seems very stupid." In other photos, Eleanor is seated on her handsome father's lap, his arm wrapped around her as she clings to him and burrows her face into his strong chest. But even for her father, Eleanor does not smile.

When Eleanor was two years old, her parents took her to the Hyde Park estate of James Roosevelt Sr., a businessman and horse breeder who served as the small town's supervisor, and his wife Sara Ann Delano Roosevelt, who had given birth to Franklin Delano Roosevelt on January 30, 1882, and asked Elliott and Anna to serve as his godparents. Sara had labored for twenty-four hours to produce her only child. The doctor had needed to breathe life into Franklin's body. As a child, he could be personable and charming, but also withdrawn, shy with strangers, and appeared to have no friends his age in whom he could confide. Although much loved by his parents, he learned to keep his own counsel.

From birth to death Franklin and Eleanor would be entangled in the family web, and not just any family, but *the*

Roosevelts, a tribal clan who taught their children that Victorian principles, which extolled the importance of hard work and ambition, would lead to success. Yet Eleanor grew up terrified of being who she was and afraid to make even the smallest mistake. On the day that offered her first sight of her fifth cousin once removed, Eleanor wore a prim white frock. "I am told," she later wrote, "that Franklin, probably under protest, crawled around the nursery (which has since been our children's), bearing me on his back."

In Lash's notes from his interviews with Dr. Viola Bernard, it was the psychiatrist's view that Eleanor unknowingly projected her father onto Franklin. "The fact that FDR was the godson of her father would have made him immediately attractive to her and encouraged her to endow him with qualities she ascribed to her father," Lash wrote. "Her attachment to her father must have impaired her ability to love any man fully—i.e. sexually." Eleanor would have been bewildered by Bernard's assessment, but she would not have been the first woman to unconsciously choose a husband much like her father. Over the years, as Anna and Elliott's marriage unraveled, it was Eleanor, not her mother, who became her father's source of affection. Eleanor later remembered that her father "was the only person who did not treat me as a criminal!" She and Elliott formed a "secret pact," where father and daughter would be left alone forever to "live in a dream world where I was the heroine and my father was the hero. . . . Into this world I withdrew."

CHAPTER 2

The Hard Years

In the long run we shape our lives and we shape ourselves.
The process never ends until we die.
—Eleanor Roosevelt

In the spring of 1887, Elliott grew nervous and moody. The reason was clear to everyone but himself. He was a chronic alcoholic with no one around him who could help set him straight. In 1888 Elliott became so drunk on one occasion that he fell from a trapeze and broke his ankle. To bear the pain, Elliot drank laudanum, a bitter-tasting tincture of opium and morphine, and had hallucinations that made him behave like a madman. In 1890 he threatened suicide and lost his job in Manhattan. His drinking put a strain on Anna, who tried to cover up his problems around relatives and friends and decided it might be a good idea to take a long trip to Europe.

In May 1887, Anna, Elliott, and two-year-old Eleanor boarded the *Britannic* and set sail for Europe. A nurse who spoke only French came along as well, which helps explain why French had been Eleanor's first language. On the first day at sea, the *Britannic* was rammed by an incoming steamer, the *Celtic*. New York newspapers reported that the prow of the *Celtic* struck the *Britannic*, glanced off, and then struck again. Many passengers were killed and others were injured. Elliott and his wife got into a lifeboat and then he asked a crewman to drop young Eleanor into his arms. Fortunately the sea was calm, but the lifeboats still pitched and people wept. Later Eleanor remembered the frantic "cries of terror" and "wild confusion." She and her parents were rowed to the *Celtic* and sailed back to New York, the family trip aborted.

Back in New York, Eleanor and her French nurse were left with one of Elliott's favorite aunts, Annie Gracie, and her husband, James King Gracie, in Oyster Bay. Elliott and Anna took the next ship to England without their daughter. Eleanor felt that somehow she was to blame for the abandonment, not her parents. If she had not been afraid, if she had jumped when her father called out to her and not made a scene, her parents would not have left her behind, she thought. As Joseph Lash wrote, "Desertion of the young and defenseless remained an ever-present theme—in her reading and her composition in school, the mere suspicion that someone she loved might have turned away from her always caused the same taut, hopeless bewilderment." Eleanor called these her "Griselda moods."

In 1890, Elliott took Anna and their two children, Eleanor and her younger brother, Elliott Jr., or Ellie, to Europe. (Their third child and second son, Gracie Hall

Roosevelt, or Hall, would be born the following year.) Teddy worried that Elliott's drinking would be picked up by the newspapers and cause a public scandal, which would have damaged Teddy's political aspirations. He wrote long letters to Elliott demanding that he pull himself together, which infuriated his younger brother. In June 1890, Anna became pregnant with Hall, and wrote to Bamie asking her sister-in-law to come to Vienna to help manage Elliott and the children. Bamie, a constant support to her brothers and to Anna, traveled to Vienna, where she took Elliott to a sanitarium and stayed by his side for his treatment for alcoholism.

Teddy believed that Elliott's obsession with alcohol might be hereditary. After Eleanor was born, Teddy told his brother that he should not have any more children because he worried that the children would grow up to become alcoholics. (Later in life, Hall did, in fact, drink himself to death.) Eleanor, however, loathed the sight of a drink. In her autobiography *This Is My Story*, published in 1937, Eleanor wrote about her brother's death and how drink affected most of the people around her. She abhorred cocktail parties with friends. She kept busy instead, recharging herself by never stopping her work.

Meanwhile, back in 1891 in New York, Teddy learned that Katy Mann, a servant employed by Anna and Elliott, had filed a paternity suit in which she claimed that she and Elliott had had an affair and that Katy had borne his child. Elliott denied the charges; Teddy vacillated between believing Mann and believing Elliott's denials, but worried that if the story was true the family name and his own political career would be destroyed. He decided finally that the family had to stand by Elliott. In his next letter to Bamie, he said that if they wanted to avoid a scandal, they had to hold to the line that they believed Elliott was innocent. "Of course," Teddy wrote, even if Elliott did do it, "he was insane when he did."

Teddy attempted to reach a settlement with Mann, but she did not back down and threatened a lawsuit. "We regard it as mere blackmail," Teddy told Bamie, "but remember what a hideous tale of his life we should have to testify to if we put him on the stand." Mann's attorney asked for $10,000, an enormous sum equivalent to about $300,000 today, that astounded Teddy. Negotiations came to a standstill until Teddy sent a detective to investigate. The detective walked the streets of Brooklyn where Mann lived, and one day he saw the child. The detective was convinced by the boy's likeness to Elliott that Mann's story was true. She named her son Elliott Roosevelt Mann, and he lived the rest of his life in New York.

With Anna's permission, Teddy and Bamie then filed a lawsuit to have Elliott declared insane and unable to care for himself. In their affidavits, his brother and sister described the deterioration of Elliot's mind, as reflected in irrational behavior. Three times, he tried to commit suicide. Teddy arranged for the value of Elliott's property, estimated at $175,000 ($5 million by today's standards), to be placed in trust for Anna and the children. The scandal to the Roosevelt name that Teddy had long dreaded broke on April 8, 1892, when *The New York Herald* screamed, "Elliott Roosevelt Demented by Excess. Wrecked by Liquor and Folly, He Is Now Confined in an Asylum for the Insane near Paris."

Elliott returned to America a broken man. His wife and his sister were afraid of him. He agreed to travel to Dwight, Illinois, for five weeks of another treatment to stop drinking. Afterward, Elliott lived on a mountainous property near Abingdon, Virginia, owned by his brother-in-law Douglas Robinson. As Joseph Alsop explained, the land covered a wilderness of virgin forest and thickets of laurel and was used as a place to "store family drunkards." While he was in Virginia, Elliott wrote letters to seven-year-old Eleanor and promised that when he was able, she could visit him. He also wrote to his mother-in-law, Mary Livingston Ludlow Hall, pleading to be allowed to see his wife, Anna. "Do not come," Hall wrote back.

Anna, thirty-nine years old, refused to talk to Elliott or write to him. She and her children moved to a new house at 61st Street and Madison Avenue, two blocks from Bamie's house. Anna worked hard to be a better mother than she had been for the children in their younger years. She helped Eleanor with her school lessons each day. She taught her to read and asked her to repeat verses from the Bible. In the afternoon, Anna read aloud to all three children.

In November 1892, Anna became ill after exposure to

ether during an operation and had a difficult time breathing. She soon contracted diphtheria and scarlet fever. The children were not allowed to see her. Two trained nurses and family members remained with Anna as weeks passed and she continued to deteriorate. Finally, Anna begged her mother to let her die. On December 7, she succumbed to her illnesses. Elliott was not present to witness his wife's death.

In May of the following year, Ellie died of the same disease that had killed his mother, diphtheria. Eleanor had now lost her mother, her brother, and for all practical purposes, her father, who seemed increasingly demented from alcohol. Death was all around her. To compensate, she focused solely on her father. Forty-five years after the deaths of her mother and brother, she wrote, "Death meant nothing to me, and one fact wiped out everything else—my father was back and I would see him very soon."

Elliott took nine-year-old Eleanor to the Knickerbocker Club in New York, a watering hole he knew well. The club had specific rules: women, children, and dogs were not allowed. Nonetheless, Elliott brought along his three fox terriers, asked Eleanor to wait outside for him, and handed her the leash for the dogs. Eleanor and the dogs waited for Elliott for six hours. He did not come out. Finally, the doorman took pity on her, called for a carriage, and sent Eleanor home, holding the dogs in her arms.

In the fall of 1893, Elliott changed his name and moved permanently back to New York, where he lived with a mistress at 313 West 102nd Street, near River-side Park. He rarely saw Eleanor, who was living with her maternal grandmother, Mary Hall, or Grandmother Hall. Occasionally he sent her books, and one time he sent her a puppy. He wrote letters to her and asked her to work on "all those little things that will make my dear girl so much more attractive if she attends to them, not forgetting the big ones: unselfishness, generosity, loving tenderness and cheerfulness." Those were odd words for Elliott to choose, since he had become the black sheep of the Roosevelt family. Nevertheless, Eleanor continued to have faith in him.

By August 1894, Elliott suffered regular blackouts at his apartment. Teddy went to see him and described Elliott's condition as "frightful." In a letter to their sister Bamie, Teddy wrote: "He had been drinking whole bottles of anisette and green mint, besides whole bottles of raw brandy and of champagne, sometimes half a dozen." On August 13, 1894, alone in his apartment, Elliott jumped through a window. He was not killed instantly, but died a few days later following a seizure.

Eleanor, then almost ten years old, was not allowed to attend her father's funeral. For years after his death, Eleanor tried to confront the depth of her father's madness and its effect on her, but she never succeeded. As Bernard, the child psychiatrist, explained: "Their mutual identification was expressed in the way she tried to identify with some kind of loving model in him—to be noble, brave, studious, religious, good as he wanted her to be—and that her father never succeeded in being." Eleanor had done all she could to keep her father alive and soon learned that life was awkward and difficult for her without him.

CHAPTER 3

The Making of a Heroine

It takes courage to love, but pain through love is
the purifying fire which those who live generously know.
—*Eleanor Roosevelt*

Eleanor, who was still living with Grandmother Hall in a gloomy brownstone on 37th Street in Manhattan, was now an orphan. Within two years she had lost her mother, her brother Elliott Jr., and her father.

Mrs. Hall was a fifty-year-old widow; her husband, Valentine Hall, had passed away fourteen years earlier without a will, and left his wife only common-law dower rights to his estate. Mrs. Hall had four grown children with their own problems. The girls, Edith (known as Pussie), twenty-two, and Maude, sixteen, were both striking women but unmarried and frustrated. The boys, Eleanor's uncles, were Vallie, twenty-seven, and Eddie, twenty-two, both already alcoholics.

Grandmother Hall placed Eleanor in a school for young girls taught by Frederic Roser, a professor who conducted private classes at the Twombly mansion, one of the

Vanderbilt houses, at 684 Fifth Avenue. One of Eleanor's cousins, Corinne Roosevelt, the younger sister of Theodore Roosevelt, later belittled Roser in print. "I cannot understand why on earth our mothers fell for the Roser classes. . . . I wish you could have seen Mr. Roser. A Prince Albert coat. Side whiskers. Not one grain of humor. Nobody in the world as pompous as he."

Eleanor was eager to learn Roser's rules, which followed the traditions of English public schools. She stood with the other girls when Roser came into the classroom, waiting for the professor to bow formally and show when they could be seated. Eleanor was devoted to literature and a serious student. In a single day, she memorized Alfred, Lord Tennyson's "The Revenge: A Ballad of the Fleet," and Roser had her recite the poem in class. The poem describes a British hero, Sir Richard Grenville, who faced down a fleet of fifty-three Spanish warships in the Battle of Flores in 1591. Sir Richard died in the battle, but what must have caught Eleanor's imagination was the courage of Sir Richard. It was the same spirit that she projected onto her father and that she longed for in her own life. Her mother had seen her as unattractive and bad tempered, but her father filled her with visions of a fairy-tale life of heroism. Eleanor, one might say, fell under the spell of what Carl Jung called "the participation mystique," which describes a person who fantasizes and holds on to illusions. The theory is that if a child does not feel loved and seen by her mother at birth, the child becomes lost and struggles to develop a strong sense of self. Eleanor's childhood fit the theory.

It was her grandmother's routine to spend winters in the house in Manhattan and summers at the Hall family estate north of the small village of Tivoli, New York, named Oak Terrace, where a stone gatehouse led to a road that passed by large stables and onto a lawn shaded by towering oaks. The mansion was a high-ceilinged, drafty house with a dining room, a music room, and a large library on the first floor and fourteen bedrooms upstairs. Eleanor's bedroom lay on the second floor.

Eleanor enjoyed the changes of the seasons, the walks in the woods, and the light on the Hudson River. Later in her life, she wrote that at Oak Terrace she spent hours reading books from the library, catching tadpoles with her brother Hall, and "there was nothing that gave me greater joy than to get one of my young aunts to agree that she would get up before dawn, that we would walk down through the woods to the river, row ourselves the five miles to the village in Tivoli to get the mail, and row back before the family was at the breakfast table."

By the time she was fifteen, Eleanor was almost six feet tall without her shoes on, and bone thin. In today's world, she might have been labeled as suffering from an eating disorder. Eleanor was self-conscious about her unconventional appearance, and felt ashamed of her body, and was afraid to make her feelings clear to those around her. The average height for most girls in 1900 was five feet, one-and-a-half inches. Eleanor's skirts were too short and her few dresses hung shapelessly on her emaciated frame. To finish it off, she wore old-fashioned black stockings with high button shoes. She became increasingly shy and avoided crowds. Often teased by boys, who made fun of her height, she stayed away from them in public places.

To compensate, Eleanor kept her head and shoulders down in a failed attempt to force herself to look smaller. Her grandmother insisted Eleanor walk up and down streets with a stick behind her shoulders, but try as she did, her shoulders stayed slouched. In one of Roser's classes in Manhattan, Eleanor wrote an essay entitled "Loyalty and Friendship," which revealed her own perception of herself. "It may seem strange but no matter how plain a woman may be if truth & loyalty are stamped on her face all will be attracted to her & those who know her will always love her for they will feel her loyal spirit & have confidence in her," Eleanor wrote.

It was her father's independent sister, Bamie, known as Aunt Bye, who realized that Eleanor needed to leave Tivoli, New York, in order to find herself and to experience the larger world. Years before, in 1869, Bye had been sent abroad to be educated by Marie Souvestre, a noted feminist and educated Frenchwoman who was headmistress of Les Ruches in Fontainebleau, near Paris. Later, Souvestre started a private finishing school called Allenswood Boarding Academy in Wimbledon, outside London. Aunt Bye decided that Eleanor needed the freedom that Allenswood offered and convinced Grandmother Hall to send her. "Your mother wanted you to go to boarding school in Europe," Grandmother Hall told Eleanor. "And I have decided to send you."

When Eleanor arrived at Allenswood, Souvestre was sixty-nine years old. Her hair was thick, wavy, and white. Her face was attractive, and Eleanor later wrote that her bright blue eyes could "look through you." She was one of only forty girls enrolled in the school. Many spoke English; however, Souvestre insisted that both inside and outside the classroom they must speak only French. One of Eleanor's classmates, Helen Gifford, later said, "I remember the day [Eleanor] came to the school, she was so very much more grown up than we were, and at her first meal, when we hardly dared open our mouths, she sat opposite Souvestre, chatting away in French." This was a moment that Eleanor would never forget.

In her first letter to Eleanor's Grandmother Hall, Souvestre told her that Eleanor had quickly become the leader of the girls in the school. "She is full of sympathy for all those who live with her and shows an intelligent interest in everything she comes in contact with," wrote Souvestre. "As a pupil she is very satisfactory, but even that is of small account when you compare it with the perfect quality of her soul."

If Grandmother Hall had known what kind of woman Souvestre was, Eleanor would no doubt have been summoned home in the first term. Souvestre's circle of friends included Henry James, Marcel Proust, the socialist reformers Sidney and Beatrice Webb, and Sir Leslie Stephen, the father of Virginia Woolf, and she made no secret of the fact that she was both an atheist and a lesbian.

Eleanor's first boarding school roommate was Marjorie Bennett, an English girl who quickly showed Eleanor around. The girls wore long skirts, usually black, white blouses, and British boaters out of doors. They made their own beds, and drawers and closets were carefully arranged. After breakfast, they took brisk walks in the English countryside. After lunch, they had tea and discussed ideas in French. Two hours of exercise was mandatory. Eleanor, who had never exercised at home, went out for field hockey. "It was one of the proudest moments of my life," she later wrote. "I liked playing with a team. It was a rough enough game, with many hard knocks."

In almost no time, Souvestre piled on the adoration for Eleanor that her mother had neglected. She nicknamed her "Totty" and pushed her to gain self-confidence, to think out loud about her aspirations, to hold nothing back, and to never give up on herself. In her first year at the school, it was Eleanor who led the conversations with the other girls at the dinner table, where she sat opposite the headmistress every evening. They discussed how education would lead to the chance of women getting the right to vote. They talked about socialism, and worried about the threat of war. After dinner, Souvestre read aloud French poems and plays. The habit of reading aloud to friends became one that Eleanor maintained over the course of her lifetime.

At Allenswood Eleanor was no longer ashamed of being the tallest girl in class. For the first time in her life, she was proud of her body. She ate what she wanted to eat, enjoyed her tea and biscuits, and did not worry about weight. With new faith in herself, Eleanor asked Souvestre if she could recommend a Parisian dressmaker to make dresses for her. "I still remember my joy," Eleanor wrote years later, "in a particular red dress that I wore over and over." At the end of the first year, Souvestre wrote again to Eleanor's grandmother: "She is the most amiable girl I have ever met; she is nice to everybody, very eager to learn and highly interested in her work."

Despite Souvestre's age, she and Eleanor traveled through Europe together on three different occasions, visiting Florence, Rome, Pisa, Marseilles, Biarritz, and Paris. Their travels showed Eleanor that she could have fun. As Hazel Rowley noted in *Franklin and Eleanor*, once Eleanor and Souvestre "were on the train to Pisa when Souvestre, on a whim, decided they would get off to see the beaches of Alassio so they could gaze at the stars." Eleanor had never met an adult like Souvestre, who continued to encourage her to take risks.

In 1949, a novel entitled *Olivia*, written by Dorothy Strachey Bussy, a teacher at Allenswood, exploded in the bookstores. The novel described a lesbian romance between a character named Olivia (herself) and Mademoiselle Julie (Souvestre), as well as featuring the character of Laura, who resembled Eleanor. After the book was published, Bussy sent Eleanor a copy of the novel and wrote, "For Totty in memory of old days from DS." But when Eleanor was a student, Souvestre was a mother figure, not a lover. To her credit, Eleanor was not ashamed about her part in the novel and did not hide it. During her time in Allenswood, she had been exposed to lesbian life and never saw it as unusual, especially in boarding schools.

Eleanor was seventeen during her third year at Souvestre's school when her Grandmother Hall learned that Eleanor had been unchaperoned in a European city and demanded that she come home to prepare to become a New York debutante. Eleanor's first cousin Corrine Douglas Robinson, whose first term at Allenswood overlapped with Eleanor's last, said that when she arrived at the school, Eleanor was "everything" at the school. Eleanor wrote: "She [Corrine] became one of the people whom I cared most for in the world, and the long separation seemed very hard to bear."

While Eleanor was back in New York, she and Souvestre maintained a correspondence until the teacher's death in March 1905. For the rest of her life Eleanor kept the letters her mentor had sent beside her father's letters, and a photograph of Souvestre stayed on her desk in New York.

That summer of 1901–1902 in Tivoli was stressful in every respect. Her two uncles, Eddie and Vallie, drank liquor night and day. Once, Vallie positioned himself at an upstairs window and fired a shotgun at his family on the lawn. Eleanor and her brother Hall took refuge behind the trees. The spectacle of her two uncles brought back memories of her father's drinking and his ultimate death. In the house in Tivoli, Eleanor's grandmother had three heavy locks placed on Eleanor's door. Her room in Manhattan had also been secured by locks. Her grandmother knew to lock those doors in order protect Eleanor, but she and Eleanor never had a conversation as to why.

One night a school friend, Laura Chandler White, spent the night with Eleanor on 37th Street, and asked why the door was bolted. "To keep my uncles out," Eleanor replied. Fear had left her at Allenswood with Madame Souvestre, but under her grandmother's roof, she had ample reason to be worried. Though locks protected her behind bedroom doors, Eleanor had to defend herself in the rest of the house, always on alert that she might be trapped by her uncles. Eleanor never acknowledged in words that she was physically abused by the two men, but she made no secret that she was terrified of them. She invited Franklin to Tivoli to protect her and keep an eye on Vallie and Eddie, and apparently when he was there, Eleanor's uncles were on their best behavior. "Vallie has been exemplary—I seem to have a good effect on him," Franklin wrote in his diary.

CHAPTER 4

The Dream of Love

The future belongs to those who believe
in the beauty of their dreams.
—Eleanor Roosevelt

Eleanor made her debut in New York at the Assembly Ball, held in the Waldorf-Astoria Hotel on December 11, 1902. A week before, the newspaper *Town Topics* had written a story about the beauty of Eleanor's mother, Anna, and the importance of her civic leadership. Eleanor found it difficult to escape her late mother's overwhelming reputation. On the evening of her debut, Eleanor was slim and stood tall in a white gown purchased from a Paris fashion design house. She appeared with four other Roosevelt debutantes, including Alice Roosevelt, the daughter of Eleanor's godfather, Teddy, who was by then the president of the United States. *Town Topics* described the Roosevelt women as "the magic Five" and "interesting-looking . . . but they are not pretty."

There were other humiliations for Eleanor. As a debutante, she was required to dance at every ball of the season and obligated to wear a dance card on her wrist. Eleanor was taller than most of the men and dreaded the debutante dances. She knew only two unmarried men, both older than she, and felt shaky when she was called on to dance with them. "I did not think I quite realized beforehand what utter agony it was going to be or I would never have had the courage to go," Eleanor wrote later. "By no stretch of the imagination could I fool myself into thinking that I was a popular debutante! I went home early, thankful to get away."

Eleanor remembered a conversation with Madame Souvestre about her longing to start "a new life," free of the troubles of her childhood. Her three years in Allens-wood, she later wrote, had "started me on my way to self-confidence." Now she was back in New York, sur-rounded by the world of debutante balls. "Protect yourself to some extent against it, my dear child," Souvestre wrote to her. "Even when success comes, as I am sure it will, bear in mind that there are more quiet and enviable joys than to be among the most sought-after-women at a ball."

In New York, Eleanor searched for new experiences with women beyond the debutantes of high society—behavior that presaged later ventures to be exposed to new and different people. It was Bob Ferguson, one of the male partners on Eleanor's dance card, who introduced her to Ellen "Bay" Emmet, an artist who maintained a studio in Greenwich Village. The two became friends. Bay was de-scended from revolutionary Irish heroes. She was plump, had bobbed red hair, wore owlish glasses, and was as far away from a debutante as Eleanor could find. Emmet had studied as a painter and illustrator in Boston, New York, and Paris. Eleanor admired her not only for her paintings but also for the group of freethinkers that gathered around the painter in her studio.

Although Eleanor did not yet understand the confusion and the promise of New York, Emmet reminded her of the many conversations Eleanor had had with Souvestre about broadening her horizons and she set out to learn more about the city. Emmet and her women friends—teachers, lawyers, educators, as well as painters—had found their own meaningful lives in Greenwich Village. In time, Eleanor would also find her authentic self in the Village.

In the summer of 1902 on a New York Central train up the Hudson River to her grandmother's home in Tivoli, Eleanor was seated in coach class with her head down in a book when Franklin walked by and saw her. Aside from his trip to Tivoli, it had been four years since the two of them had last encountered each other. He sat down and they talked for almost two hours. Franklin then took Eleanor to another parlor car where his mother, Sara Delano Roosevelt, sat dressed in black with heavy mourning veils that fell to the ground. Sara's husband James Roosevelt had died of a heart attack two years before and she was still in mourning.

Eleanor began seeing Franklin at dinner parties and dances. They were now about the same height, at six feet tall, and literally saw each other eye to eye as they danced around the room. Franklin told Eleanor that she was not only beautiful but that he liked her because she was smart. The two discussed their interest in philosophy, ethics, poetry, and the events of the day. Franklin invited her to Harvard in the fall, for dances and football games. She agreed, and they also spent time with Franklin's family in Hyde Park in the Hudson Valley of New York, wandering in the stables and along the walking trails, through the many beautiful gardens. Franklin had the habit of writing in code in his journal, substituting numbers for vowels and squiggles for consonants. He did that to keep his secrets from his prying mother, Sara Delano Roosevelt. That Christmas a translation of his secret code would have read: "E is an Angel." While Eleanor's early life had been grim, Franklin's appeared to have been idyllic. He was born on January 30, 1882. His father, "Mr. James," was a country gentleman, a lawyer and farmer of considerable wealth, who had been fifty-two years old, twice her age, when he married Franklin's mother, Sara, with her large brown eyes and lustrous hair. Sara breastfed her son for a year by herself, without seeking help from her maids, as was customary at the time. She built her own world around her son. She and her husband took young Franklin to Europe many times and spent every summer with him on Campobello Island, off the coast of New Brunswick in Canada. Like Teddy, Franklin had a stamp collection, loved collecting birds, and enjoyed taking boats out onto the water.

At home in Hyde Park, every moment of every day was structured. At 8 a.m. Franklin had breakfast, and from nine o'clock to noon, he worked with tutors. He had one hour of play before lunch, which came at one o'clock. There were no more lessons until four, and dinner was at 6 p.m. He went to his bedroom at eight o'clock. "No moment of Franklin's day was unscheduled," Roosevelt biographer Geoffrey C. Ward has written. "His mother oversaw everything, followed him everywhere. . . . Hers was a loving adoring autocracy but an autocracy nonetheless."

When Franklin sought out privacy, Sara felt shunned. In a memoir, *My Boy Franklin*, written late in Sara's life, FDR's mother acknowledged that she might have smothered her son:

> We never tried . . . his father and I, to influence him against his own tastes and inclinations or to shape his life. At least we made every effort not to and thought we were succeeding pretty well until one day . . . we noticed that he seemed much depressed. . . . Finally, a little alarmed, I asked him whether he was unhappy. He did not answer at once and then said very seriously, "Yes I am unhappy." When I asked him, he was silent for a moment or two. Then with a curious little gesture that combined entreaty with a suggestion of impatience, he clasped his hands in front of him and exclaimed, "Oh for freedom!"

As the New Year approached, Eleanor and Franklin were both invited to the White House, where Uncle Teddy served as president. Eleanor spent the night there with her cousin Alice. Franklin stayed at Aunt Bye's home. Bamie (Aunt Bye) was her brother Teddy's strongest advocate and adviser, and her house at 1733 N Street became known in Washington as the "Little White House." Teddy often used that house to meet with friends and individuals whom, for personal reasons, he preferred not to invite to the White House. That night Teddy placed Franklin in Bamie's house to allow him distance from Alice, who thrived on being the center of attention as the "First Daughter," and who had an eye for her cousin.

During dinner, however, Franklin sat next to Teddy, and enjoyed talking to the president. Franklin was already enamored of politics and hoped to one day follow Teddy into the power of the presidency. Eleanor, in turn, had been surrounded by powerful men—her grandfathers and her uncle Teddy—and now she was caught up in her love for Franklin and his love for her. After the meal, the younger group went into the White House theater for a party. Later Franklin noted in his diary: "sat near Eleanor. . . . Very interesting day."

Eleanor visited Cambridge on November 21, 1903, for the Harvard-Yale football game. The next day they went to Groton to visit Eleanor's brother Hall. During that visit, Franklin proposed to Eleanor, who immediately said yes. Afterward, Franklin wrote (in code): "After lunch I had a never to be forgotten walk with my darling."

Sara did not approve. She told Franklin that he and Eleanor were too young to marry. How, asked Sara, would he support a wife and, presumably, children? Franklin reminded her that he had a trust fund from his father's estate that provided $5,000 a year and that Eleanor had a similar fund that yielded $7,500 a year. Sara said Franklin would need more money than that to finish his degree from Harvard and then to start law school.

By way of a solution, Sara suggested a deal with her son. She insisted he and Eleanor keep their engagement a secret for a year. If they felt the same way about each other in a year's time, Sara said she would approve of the marriage. When Eleanor received the news, she sent Franklin a letter on Sunday, December 13, that said: "Whatever you do I shall know it to be right but I don't quite think your Mother quite realizes what a very hard thing she was asking me to do for I am hungry for every moment of your time." To satisfy Sara, Franklin took the deal.

In that year, Franklin finished his studies at Harvard, and Eleanor found a job at the Rivington Street settlement house in New York's Lower East Side. To her credit, Eleanor remembered that her goal in life was to expand the lives of others. She and one of her friends, Jean Reid, taught dance and calisthenics to immigrant girls—mostly Jews and Italians—who lived in the squalid tenements of the city. Eleanor admired the girls they taught for attending dance classes after a hard day's labor in factories or doing piecework at home.

At the end of an evening of teaching, Jean offered Eleanor a ride home in her carriage, but Eleanor decided she would take the trip uptown by public transportation, like other ordinary New Yorkers. Sometimes she took the elevated train and other times she rode the Fourth Avenue streetcar. Either way, she had to walk through the Bowery, where she saw many men come out of saloons or shabby hotels. Once again Eleanor saw the consequences of alcoholism and feared it. As she looked at the unkempt men, she remembered that her father had once taken her to a clubhouse for newsboys and Eleanor had found herself, as she later put it, "tremendously interested in all these ragged little boys and in the fact which my father explained, that many of them had no homes and lived in wooden shanties."

On a day when Franklin was in New York, Eleanor asked him to stop by Rivington Street. One of the immigrant girls was sick, and Eleanor asked Franklin to help her take the child to the dilapidated tenement where she lived. The sour smells and gruff sounds in the small space horrified Franklin. "My God," he told Eleanor, "I didn't know anyone lived like that." This firsthand experience of poverty would influence him in later years, and it was Eleanor who had initiated it. She would do this often for him throughout his life: steer him toward problems in the world that needed addressing. As difficult as her childhood was, it had given Eleanor great strength. "We do not have to be heroes overnight," she once wrote. "Instead, just a step at a time, meeting each thing that comes up, seeing it as dreadful as it appears, discovering that we have the strength to stare it down."

THE DREAM OF LOVE

Franklin's life continued to be complicated by his mother's interference. He was calm and focused, but he always looked over his shoulder to flee Sara, who not only had postponed his marriage but kept him on an allowance until 1941. Eleanor wrote love letters to Franklin to keep up his spirit and her own. "It's impossible to tell you what these last two days have been to me," she wrote after one visit to Hyde Park, "but I know they have meant the same to you so that you will understand that I love you dearest and I hope that I shall always prove worthy of the love you have given me. I have never before known what it was to be absolutely happy."

She thrived on her experience of falling in love. "Oh! Darling I miss you so and I long for the happy hours which we have together. . . . I am so happy," she wrote in January 1904. "So *very* happy in your love dearest, that all the world has changed for me. If only I can bring to you all that you have brought to me all my dearest wishes will be fulfilled and I shall know that you too will always be happy."

On October 11, 1904, Eleanor's twentieth birthday, Franklin gave her a diamond engagement ring from Tiffany in New York. Sara had failed to break up their romance, and on December 1, 1904, the engagement was formally announced. "President's Niece to Wed Her Cousin," various newspapers reported.

Teddy, who planned to give Eleanor away, wrote a note to Franklin and said: "We are greatly rejoiced over the good news. I am as fond of Eleanor as if she were my daughter; and I like you, and trust you, and believe in you." On November 8, 1904, Teddy won reelection as president by the largest majority in American history up to that time. Franklin and Eleanor came to Washington to hear his inaugural address (March 4, 1905), and the young couple danced that night at the inaugural ball, without thought that one day they, too, would be living in the White House.

CHAPTER 5

Wife and Mother

You wouldn't worry so much about what others think of you
if you realized how seldom they do.
—*Eleanor Roosevelt*

Eleanor and Franklin were married on St. Patrick's Day, March 17, 1905, by an American Episcopal priest, Endicott Peabody, who had founded the Groton School for Boys, where Franklin had gone to school (1896–1900). Later in his life, FDR said that Peabody had influenced him more than anyone except his father and mother. The marriage took place on 76th Street in New York City, the home of Eleanor's cousin and godmother, Susan Ludlow Parish. Eleanor was twenty years old and Franklin, twenty-three.

In the days prior to the wedding, Eleanor curiously adopted her finicky mother's upper-class notions of Victorian proprieties—such as attending parties and accepting gifts as part of the rituals of an engagement—the very ideas she had disdained previously. There were 340 gifts in all— candlesticks, tea sets, four inkstands, and thirteen clocks.

Eleanor received a lot of jewelry, including a collar with diamond bars that was a gift from her soon-to-be mother-in-law, Sara. Franklin gave Eleanor a gold watch pin etched with her initials in diamonds. He gave his best man and his groomsmen lapel pins featuring the Roosevelt family insignia, of which he was always proud, three feathers above a cluster of roses.

There were traces of winter on that day, but Midtown Manhattan was crowded with spectators who held both American and Irish flags. Some strutted as they marched with fiddles and drums to the tune of "The Wearin' of the Green." Teddy, whose second term's inauguration had taken place two weeks earlier, would have been there anyway, to enjoy New York's St. Patrick's Day Parade. He wore a shamrock in his lapel and tipped his top hat to the cheering crowd. But the president had come for a second, more special reason: to give away his niece Eleanor on her wedding day. At 3:30 p.m., Teddy and his wife, Edith, arrived on 76th Street, and the wedding began.

An altar had been set up in front of the mantel in the drawing room where Eleanor and Franklin would be married. Eleanor and her six bridesmaids, including Alice Roosevelt, dressed on the third floor. Downstairs, Eleanor's Grandmother Hall was already seated, arms on her lap, as was Franklin's mother, Sara. When the musicians struck up the wedding march, the bridesmaids moved step by step down the circular stairway and up the aisle.

On the arm of her uncle, Eleanor walked toward Franklin, who stood tall at the altar. A few of the guests gasped at the sight of Eleanor, who looked surprisingly like the very image of her deceased mother, Anna, who had been born on this very day in 1863. Given Eleanor's mistreatment by her mother, it seemed unusual that she chose that date to be married, but many times in Eleanor's lost childhood and girlhood, she had thought of what it would be like to not just be ordinary but beautiful, so beautiful that even her mother would see her daughter as a shining, blissful, happy woman, so perhaps that influenced her decision. Eleanor wore a white satin dress covered in rose-point lace that her grandmother and her mother had worn at their weddings. The veil that covered her hair was secured with a diamond crescent also worn by her mother. For the first time in Eleanor's life, newspaper reporters wrote that she was "beautiful," "regal," "magnificent."

When the Reverend Peabody asked at the altar, "Who giveth this woman in marriage?" Teddy smiled and roared "I do!" Eleanor and Franklin exchanged vows, gave each other a ring, and the crowd stood still for the kiss. Eleanor was taller than Teddy, who had to stand on his toes to hug her. When he turned to Franklin, Teddy said: "Well, Franklin, there's nothing like keeping the name in the family." The next morning, the *New York Times* society pages weighed in on the event: "The wedding of Miss Eleanor Roosevelt and Franklin Delano Roosevelt, her cousin, took on the semblance of a National 'Event,'" with one observer stating that "the entire family in every degree of cousinship, made it very much like a 'royal alliance.'" The *Times* continued, "The President is never so happy as when he is one of the chief actors in a great family gathering."

At 5 p.m., Teddy's carriage departed and turned left toward Fifth Avenue, which was jammed with people reaching out to try to touch or at least get a look at the president and his wife. Eleanor and Franklin briefly said hello to their friends and then made their way to Grand Central Terminal, where they took the train to Franklin's family home in Hyde Park for the beginning of their honeymoon. A coachman met them at the small station in Hyde Park, and took them up the long drive, where they were greeted by Elespie McEachern, the Scottish caretaker who ran a spotless household for Sara. (In 1881 McEachern had also welcomed Sara as a new bride when she arrived with Franklin's father, James.) Eleanor, the new Mrs. Roosevelt, later wrote that Elespie "looked me over critically and appraisingly, wondering if I could come up to her expectations."

Franklin's choice to spend the wedding night in his mother's house was problematic for Eleanor. The house was filled with Sara's belongings, and she heard the footsteps of the staff, not to mention their whisperings about the wedding night. Franklin was comfortable in the house where he was born and wasn't worried about the wedding night, since he had apparently been well schooled in sex. In diaries written in 1902, Franklin wrote that he had dated no fewer than a dozen girls. He was serious about at least one of them, Alice Sohier, the seventeen-year-old daughter of a wealthy family in Boston. They went swimming together at the beach and did some serious "petting," as physical intimacy short of intercourse quaintly used to be called. Both worried that they had gone too far. In one of his diaries, Franklin wrote: "Spend evening on lawn. Alice confides in her doctor." Franklin had asked Alice to marry him, but she decided against it. Fifty years after the night on the beach, Alice Sohier told her granddaughter, "In a day and age when well brought-up young men were expected to keep their hands off the person of young ladies from respectable families, Franklin had to be slapped—*hard.*"

No wonder Eleanor worried that she would be inadequate to meet Franklin's needs in bed. As a born Victorian, Eleanor knew little about sex, but she did understand her obligations as a young wife. She had been expected to stay a virgin until her wedding night and then go along with whatever Franklin wanted. Her cousin Alice had experience with many boyfriends and was more of an expert. When the two of them were in their early teens, Alice attempted to tell Eleanor some of the facts of life. "I almost came to grief," Alice recalled. "She suddenly leapt on me and tried to sit on my head and smothered me with a pillow, saying I was being blasphemous. So I shut up and I think she probably went to her wedding not knowing anything about the subject at all." No wonder that Eleanor once told her daughter Anna that sex "was an ordeal to be borne."

Their honeymoon was in Europe, where Eleanor

and Franklin spent several weeks touring Britain, France, and Germany. On the voyage home to New York, Eleanor thought she was seasick but realized she was actually pregnant. Franklin, an only child, was delighted. He told Eleanor he wanted to have many children—at least six, preferably ten.

What Eleanor wanted was a home of her own, but her mother-in-law, Sara, the omnipresent matriarch, would have none of that. While Franklin and Eleanor were abroad, Sara rented and furnished a house at 125 East 36th Street, three blocks from her own home. There was nothing left for Eleanor to do at the time but be quiet and accept Sara's orders. When Eleanor and Franklin went to Hyde Park, Sara sat at one end of a table for dinner and Franklin at the other end. There were two chairs by the fireplace for Franklin and Sara. Eleanor, for her part, sat on the floor.

Eleanor became bitter about losing her own identity to Sara. "I was growing very dependent of my mother-in-law, requiring her help on almost every subject, and never thought of asking for anything which I felt could not meet with her approval." But it was never enough, and Franklin either didn't notice Eleanor's dilemma or ignored it. The result was that Eleanor found herself trapped in Sara's shadow, which brought back memories of her own, unloving mother.

It was Sara who made preparations for the birth of Eleanor's first child, a girl named Anna Eleanor, who was born on May 3, 1906. When Eleanor had difficultly breast-feeding, Sara hired a trained nurse to bottle-feed the baby. "I had never had any interest in dolls or in little children and I knew absolutely nothing about handling or feeding a baby," Eleanor later wrote. It was Sara who put together her own nursery staff and went to great lengths to care for the six babies that Eleanor would bear during the first ten years of marriage.

In early 1907, Sara bought two houses on the north side of East 65th Street between Park and Madison Avenues and decided she would construct one building that would contain two residences, one for herself and one for Franklin and Eleanor. She hired a well-known architect, Charles Platt, to design the house, and Franklin eagerly went over the plans with Sara and the architect. When finished, the six-story Roosevelt house was neo-Georgian in style, built with buff brick and limestone trim. It had one common front entrance and interconnecting doors. The Roosevelts moved into it in the fall of 1908. As one stood facing north on East 65th, Sara's home was to the left (west) at No. 47, and Franklin and Eleanor's to the right (east) at No. 49. On each of the floors, Sara had full access to both homes; the house had been designed to allow her free passage on every level. Eleanor had no privacy and came to believe that her mother-in-law was determined that she—not Franklin and not herself—would be the head of the family. After Eleanor and her family were moved into Sara's house, Eleanor suffered from depression, which she later wrote about:

That autumn I did not quite know what was the matter with me, but I remember that a few weeks after we moved into the house in East 65th Street I sat in front of my dressing table and wept, and when my bewildered young husband asked me what on earth was the matter with me, I said I did not like to live in a house which was in no ways mine, one that I had done nothing about and which did not represent the way I wanted to live. Being an eminently reasonable person, he thought I was quite mad and told me so gently, and said I would feel different in a little while and left me alone until I should become calmer.

Eleanor continued to bear children. James Roosevelt II, named after Franklin's father, arrived in 1907. Franklin Delano Roosevelt Jr. was born in 1909. He was a big baby, full of smiles, yet in a few weeks he grew ill. The doctor found a murmur in his heart and diagnosed endocarditis, an inflammation of the inner layer of the heart. When he died that same year, Eleanor was devastated and blamed herself. "To this day," she later wrote, "I can stand by his tiny stone in the churchyard and see the little group of people gathered around his tiny coffin, and remember how cruel it seemed to leave him out there alone in the cold." She continued to wear mourning clothes for the baby while pregnant with Elliott in 1910. There were two later children—a second Franklin Delano Roosevelt Jr. in 1914, who was born at Campobello and was the first child

Eleanor breastfed, and John Aspinwall Roosevelt, born in Washington, DC, in 1916.

In the 1870s there was a brief moment when advances in condoms and diaphragms had been made available, but Congress outlawed their sale. As a young wife at the beginning of the twentieth century, the only legal option Eleanor had in avoiding pregnancy was abstinence. It took a long time for the first birth control pill, championed by Margaret Sanger, to be released. But that was not until 1960, and by then Eleanor's childbearing days were over, and she had long since embarked on a journey of self-discovery that was not about her role as a mother.

CHAPTER 6

Victorian Restraint,
Upended

You gain strength, courage and confidence by every experience
in which you really stop to look fear in the face.
You are able to say to yourself, "I lived through this horror.
I can take the next thing that comes along."
—*Eleanor Roosevelt*

In 1910, a week after the birth of his son Elliott, Franklin was nominated as the Democratic candidate for the Twenty-Sixth State Senate District in New York, as his mentor Teddy Roosevelt had been before him. Franklin was only twenty-eight years old. His district encompassed three rural counties in the Hudson Valley: Dutchess, Putnam, and Columbia, all counties that had voted Republican for the preceding thirty-two years. In those counties, Franklin often mentioned his popular Republican cousin. "I'm not Teddy," FDR told the crowds, but he made sure they knew that, like Teddy, he would end "boss rule" and "rotten corruption" in New York.

The people of the district liked Franklin's young, happy style. In 1920, men in the Hudson Valley still rode teams of horses. Franklin was the first candidate to buy himself an automobile, a two-cylinder, bright red Maxwell roadster that he named "Red Peril." The top speed for the car was twenty-two miles an hour. He gave between ten and twenty speeches each day—at crossroads and in railroad stations, post offices, and village squares. Every speech began with "My Friends!" He was not only handsome, but also smart and good-hearted. In addition, he was wealthy enough to pour $2,500 of his own money into the campaign. On November 8, 1910, FDR won the seat by a narrow margin and was on his way to political glory.

Throughout that summer, Eleanor spent time at Campobello, writing letters to Franklin, encouraging him to plunge full force into politics. Both decided it would be better to move the family to Albany, in upstate New York. Eleanor was particularly pleased, as it would be the first time in her marriage that she would not have to live in her mother-in-law's house. Sara was naturally opposed to the move. "I think I knew that it was good for me," Eleanor wrote later. "I wanted to be independent."

Despite Sara's disapproval, Eleanor made a home of her own for her family in Albany. She and Franklin rented a three-story house at 248 State Street, near the Capitol. Her newfound freedom allowed her to focus on her husband's new life in politics. In Albany, they were happy and closer to each other than they had ever been. Nothing at that time put a strain on their marriage. Franklin enjoyed the political life, and Eleanor, who had long listened to her uncle Teddy Roosevelt talk about politics, was a great help to her husband.

The day after FDR was sworn in, on New York's Day, 1911, Eleanor had 250 people to their new home for lunch. She made sure it was an open house for FDR's supporters, colleagues, and constituents. On many days, she sat in the gallery of the Capitol listening to the debates. She made a point of calling on other political wives and met with people in their own homes to lobby for causes. In the afternoon, Eleanor was home with her children, and in the evening, after dinner, she made it a practice to read aloud to them.

At this time in their marriage, FDR and Eleanor treated each other kindly, but Eleanor conformed herself to what she thought Franklin wanted her to be. For example, in 1912, Franklin, in his role as a member of the New York State Senate, announced his support for women's suffrage. He had never asked Eleanor what she thought, despite the fact that Eleanor was well aware of women and children's rights by 1912. She later said she was "somewhat shocked, as I had never given the question serious thought." Eleanor wanted to give Franklin the credit of considering women's suffrage and didn't want to steal his thunder. Franklin did not ask Eleanor to take his stand, but Eleanor decided that if her husband supported women's suffragists, she would as well.

On March 4, 1913, Eleanor and Franklin traveled to

Washington to attend Woodrow Wilson's inauguration. While they were there, Josephus Daniels, the navy secretary, offered Roosevelt the job of assistant secretary of the navy. FDR replied about the job, "I'd like it pretty well. It would please me better than anything in the world." Franklin took his oath of office a few days later, on March 7. He was once again following in the footsteps of Teddy Roosevelt, who had previously held the navy position. This new role would call for Franklin and Eleanor to relocate quickly to Washington.

March 17 was their wedding anniversary, but for the first time, Eleanor was not with Franklin. She had returned to Albany to be with her children. Franklin's new office was on the third floor of the Navy Building, on Pennsylvania Avenue, and from his desk, he wrote to Eleanor: "My own dear Babbie—I didn't know till I sat down at this desk that this is the 17th of happy memory. In fact, all the subdued excitement of getting confirmed & taking the oath of office, the delighted significance of it all is only beginning to dawn on me."

At twenty-eight years old, Eleanor had a husband she admired and children she adored, both of which made her feel complete. She also paid more attention to dressing well, and became what was then called a "Gibson Girl," the feminine ideal of the day: hair piled on the head, narrow waist, and tall, which Eleanor was proud of being for the first time in her life.

She and Franklin were ready to take Washington by

storm. They rented Aunt Bye's house at 1733 N Street, twenty minutes from the White House. By that time, Bamie was living in Connecticut. Eleanor quickly acquired a reputation as a gracious hostess, which helped her overcome her shyness. "I learned a liberating thing," she later wrote. "If you forget about yourself, whether or not you are making a good impression on people, what they think of you, and you think about them instead, you won't be shy."

Aunt Bye gave Eleanor instructions about the importance for Washington political wives to go "calling." Most afternoons Eleanor left her calling card at the door of cabinet wives, congressional wives, and Supreme Court wives. If the women couldn't come to the door, Eleanor was free to leave. If the women came to the door, she saw them face-to-face. Eleanor kept a detailed log of women she met so that she could show it to Franklin.

By this time, with the children—Anna, James, and Elliot (and later two more)—plus four servants, a nurse, and a governess, it was a busy, crowded house. Eleanor decided she needed a social secretary to help manage her obligations, and in the winter of 1914, she hired Lucy Page Mercer. When Lucy Mercer came into the Roosevelts' family life, she was twenty-two years old, fair, slender, and attractive. She worked three mornings a week and was paid $30 a week. The children adored her, and Eleanor found her reliable and cheerful. Lucy's parents, Carroll and Minnie Mercer, had once lived on N Street, next door to Bamie's home. Carroll had fought alongside Teddy with the Rough

Riders in Cuba. While Lucy was still a young girl, her father, an alcoholic, had divorced his wife.

On March 13, 1916, Eleanor gave birth to her last child, John Aspinwall Roosevelt, and that summer, she traveled to Campobello with her children. While Eleanor was away, Franklin and Lucy began an affair. Lucy later told a friend that from the time that they met, she and Franklin were "inexorably drawn to each other." In June 1917, Lucy stopped working for Eleanor. Franklin had encouraged her to enlist as a female yeoman in the navy, which she did, and as he was the assistant secretary in the navy, their access to each other soon became unlimited.

Franklin's attention to Lucy was evident to almost everyone—except Eleanor. He took Lucy for cruises on navy yachts and for long drives in the country. His daughter, Anna, knew about the affair, but kept the secret from her mother because Anna idolized Lucy. (Imagine Eleanor's despair when she eventually learned of Anna's support for Lucy.) Alice Roosevelt, Eleanor's cousin and maid of honor when she and Franklin were married, also took Lucy's side. Alice had always been jealous of Eleanor and, in fact, encouraged the affair between Lucy and Franklin. That summer Alice invited Franklin and Lucy to dinner parties, and that promoted their romance. Franklin no longer tried to hide the affair. "I saw you twenty miles out in the country," Alice told Franklin. "You didn't see me. Your hands were on the wheel, but your eyes were on that perfectly lovely lady."

During 1917–18, Eleanor and Franklin saw little of

each other. America had entered the First World War, and Eleanor sent her children to her mother-in-law in Hyde Park and devoted herself to the war effort. She made daily rounds in her Red Cross uniform and prepared for troop trains carrying wounded soldiers scheduled to arrive in the Washington railroad yards. Eleanor worked long shifts and was good at details. The work took her mind off the general challenges of her life. She was raising children on her own, as Franklin was often at work in Washington. Instead, she focused on wounded sailors and their families, providing them soup, coffee, and sandwiches. The families were in so much need. Eleanor also gave money, and her friends followed her example. Soon she had raised funding for a recreational center for wounded men who needed physical therapy. Eleanor was especially proud that in July 1918, her uncle, Teddy, distributed money from his Nobel Peace Prize among those people and organizations who were doing the most to help. The largest sum went to the Red Cross, $6,900, and $5,000 went to his niece Eleanor to continue her charity work.

In July 1918, Franklin was sent to Europe to oversee naval facilities and crossed the Atlantic on a destroyer. The weather was stormy and the seas rough. At one point, the destroyer almost collided with another convoy. When the weather calmed, Franklin wrote to Eleanor and said: "We must come over here when the world is safe again, but I will not ask you to try a destroyer, though I have loved every minute of it."

Eleanor traveled back and forth from Washington to Hyde Park to be with her children. She missed Franklin and was worried about the impact his possible lack of love for her would have on the children.

On September 12, 1918, while at Hyde Park, Eleanor received a telegram. Franklin had returned to New York City from a trip to France on a navy destroyer. During the sail home, he had contracted double pneumonia. Eleanor, Sara, and the children quickly returned to New York. It took four navy orderlies to carry Franklin on a stretcher from the ambulance to Sara's house on East 65th Street in Manhattan. Eleanor was worried, not just for Franklin, but for her children, who adored their father.

By then the Spanish influenza epidemic of 1918 had swept the country. That night Franklin tossed in bed with a high fever and Eleanor stayed beside him. The following morning, while unpacking Franklin's suitcase, she discovered a bundle of love letters from Lucy Mercer. "The bottom dropped out of my own particular world & I faced myself, my surroundings, my world, honestly for the first time," Eleanor later wrote. She had ignored any gossip about Franklin and Lucy. Franklin's love for Eleanor had been the key that gave her self-confidence and self-respect, and now that was gone. Eleanor felt that his love for Lucy had betrayed her own sexuality. Her body had been reduced to its biological use; meant only to produce children and give Franklin the large family he wanted.

Eleanor went to Franklin's bedside and confronted him

with the letters, which he did not repudiate. Marriages disintegrated every day, of course, even in the Victorian days that shaped Eleanor's and Franklin's upbringing, but if Franklin were to leave Eleanor for his lover Lucy, divorce would be undesirable for political and personal reasons. Nonetheless, Eleanor told Franklin she would grant him a divorce. By then, she realized that her love for Franklin and their marriage had been based on illusions that his affair with Lucy had exposed. Franklin and Eleanor went awkwardly to tell Franklin's mother. Sara told Franklin that if he insisted on leaving his wife and children she could not stop him, but if he did so she would disinherit him and not give him another cent. The threat to disinheritance was not exaggerated. Sara had the family's money as well as title to the Roosevelt family home in Hyde Park. If he divorced Eleanor, he would not inherit Hyde Park, a home he loved. Franklin had settled on a career in politics. Without his mother's financial support, he would not be able to afford to run for higher office.

Time passed, and Lucy held out hope that Franklin would leave Eleanor. Two of Lucy's female cousins later told Josephus Daniels Jr., the son of Secretary Daniels and a press secretary to Franklin, that "she and Franklin were very much in love with each other. A marriage would have taken place but as Lucy said to us 'Eleanor was not willing to step down.'" Lucy was mistaken, for Eleanor had already offered Franklin his freedom. He may have wanted that freedom, but the cost of losing his inheritance and his beloved Hyde Park proved too high a price.

In addition, there were questions about how devoted a Catholic Lucy was. Would she have married a divorced man? Would Franklin have become a Catholic? In the first volume of her book *Eleanor Roosevelt*, called *The Early Years*, Blanche Wiesen Cook offers an astute answer: "Undoubtedly too much has been made of the chilling effect of Lucy Mercer's Catholicism, since FDR was in fact the love of her life." Another reason that the marriage did not take place was that, by then, Franklin wanted to be president.

Fortunately for Franklin, these were the days of an obliging press, and news of his affair was kept secret from the public at large by Louis Howe, FDR's closest political adviser since 1911. Time went on and Eleanor was impatient. She told Franklin that if he did not break things off with Lucy, she would insist on her own divorce. The terms of reconciliation between Franklin and Eleanor were worked out with the help of Howe, who soothed Eleanor by telling her that Franklin needed her to advance his own political career. He then told FDR that a divorce would end his political life, and tried to persuade him that he needed Eleanor, not only as his wife but also as his political partner.

Franklin promised Eleanor that he would never see Lucy again, a promise he broke many times in his life. The letters from Lucy were destroyed, presumably by one of the Roosevelts or Howe, and expunged from history. In the process, their marriage was redefined, allowing each of them to have his or her own independence—both politically and personally. Their son, James Roosevelt, described the agreement as "an armed truce that endured until the day FDR died." Doris Kearns Goodwin put it another way when she wrote in her book *No Ordinary Time: Franklin and Eleanor Roosevelt: The Home Front in World War II*, "No longer did Eleanor need to define herself slowly in terms of his wants and needs. With the discovery of the affair, she was free to define a new and different partnership with her husband, free to seek new avenues of fulfillment." These new avenues would soon extend into Greenwich Village, where she found her own identity.

In January 1919, the navy sent Franklin to Europe, and he took Eleanor with him. They boarded the *George Washington* for what would be their first trip to Europe together since their honeymoon, a trip designed to see what kind of relationship the two of them would now form. While on the ship, Eleanor learned of the sudden death of her sixty-year-old uncle and godfather, Teddy Roosevelt. Late in the evening, the former president had told his wife Edith that his heart felt as if it was about to stop. A doctor checked his vital signs and found nothing amiss. Teddy drifted off to sleep, and four hours later his breath stopped and did not resume. Archie, Teddy's son, cabled his brothers: "The old lion is dead."

Eleanor and FDR had boarded the navy ship to begin an exploration of their marriage after the Lucy Mercer affair. Instead, it was the death of Teddy Roosevelt that made them each reevaluate their relationship. Franklin was now the up-and-coming patriarch of the family and would have to pick up Teddy's mantle. This task was made more difficult because of his affair with Lucy and the stress in his marriage.

Later in life, Eleanor did not talk about her struggle with Mercer—but she never forgot it. "I have the memory of an elephant," wrote Eleanor. "I can forgive but never forget." During World War I, she described her own personal ideas about forgiveness: "I think I learned then that practically no one in the world is entirely bad or entirely good, and that motives are often more important than actions," she wrote. "I had spent most of my life in an atmosphere where everyone was sure of what was right and what was wrong, and as life progressed I have gradually come to believe that human beings who try to judge human beings are undertaking a somewhat difficult job. During the war I became a more tolerant person, far less sure of my own beliefs and methods of action, but I think more determined to try for certain ultimate objectives. I knew more about the human heart, which had been somewhat veiled in mystery."

Eleanor's deepest moments of introspection came in the aftermath of her discovery of her husband's extramarital affair. She was a lifelong member of the Episcopal Church, as was Franklin. Once, their daughter, Anna, asked her mother what good it did to pray. Eleanor said, "Though the responsibility seems great I'll just do my best and trust in God." Eleanor also believed she had a spiritual connection to the natural world. She would often go on long hikes when she needed to think things through.

As her friend and biographer Joseph P. Lash wrote,

Eleanor often took refuge in Rock Creek Cemetery in Washington, sitting in front of a haunting statue of a tall, shrouded figure called *Grief,* also known as the Adams Memorial, commissioned by historian Henry Adams, the descendant of two presidents, as a grave marker for his melancholic wife, Marian, a photographer who had committed suicide by drinking a developing chemical at the age of forty-two, only eight years older than Eleanor at the time of the Lucy Mercer affair. The solitude of the cemetery afforded Eleanor the space to take charge of her life and her situation. For the rest of her life, she went back to see *Grief* in times of sadness and trouble.

In some ways, Lucy did Eleanor a favor by freeing her from the life she had imagined as a young girl, borne of life with a tragic, needy father. As a child, she had worked hard to make her father feel good about himself, and as a wife, she had done a version of the same thing with Franklin. But in the wake of Franklin and Lucy's love affair, fate gave Eleanor a new set of guiding beliefs. The marriage, as it had been, was over. Eleanor became Franklin's political partner, not his lover. Each gave the other room to be free to pursue his or her own political and personal agenda. Eleanor worked hard to leave her Victorian past and its ideals behind her and set out to find where she belonged and how her life could, at last, be her own.

CHAPTER 7

Bohemians and Prohibition
in the Village

The very thing you need to be doing is the thing
that terrifies you the most.
—*Eleanor Roosevelt*

The year 1919 in America is often noted as marking the end of World War I (though actually the Armistice was signed on November 11, 1918) and, about two weeks after the death of Theodore Roosevelt on January 6, 1919, the ratification of the Eighteenth Amendment of the Constitution, or Prohibition, which generally outlawed the manufacture, transportation, and sale of alcoholic beverages. But there were other notable events that year, including a series of workers' strikes in Seattle, Boston, and Cleveland, and anarchist bombings—all acts of protest against the entrenched power structure, stemming from a desire to critique, subvert, change, or even destroy the status quo. Crosscurrents were at work nationally and in the life of Eleanor Roosevelt, too, though she could not possibly have known where they were going to take her.

But one of those places would soon become clear: Greenwich Village. It was a place already well known for its "bohemian" culture—artistic, alternative, politically progressive—and if the Village was not waiting for Eleanor, then it certainly was available to her when she became receptive to its allure and ethos. The term "bohemian," it seems worth noting, emerged in Paris in the 1830s when a group of skilled artists, who worked in the great cathedrals, went out on their own to create whatever they wanted. The artists, along with like-minded intellectuals and rebels, were poor and gathered together in the Latin Quarter on the Left Bank, where rents were cheap. The French called them "Gypsy Bohemians" because they practiced unconventional lifestyles. The idea of the bohemian artist's life in the Latin Quarter was popularized by Henri Murger's 1851 novel (or collection of tales) *La vie de bohème*, which in 1859 Murger and a coauthor turned into a very popular play, *La vie de bohème*, which in turn inspired Puccini's *La bohème* (1896). The first prominent American to settle in bohemian Paris was James McNeill Whistler, who arrived in Paris in 1855 when he was twenty-one years old and took a studio in the Latin Quarter. In time the word came to signify a mind-set, a lifestyle of creativity and freedom.

In his book *Republic of Dreams: Greenwich Village: The American Bohemia, 1910–1960*, Ross Wetzsteon called the years in Greenwich Village between 1912 and 1917 "the lyric years," "the confident years," "the innocent revolution." Something new was happening in New York; it was the first of several golden ages of the Village. The area, mostly a collection of three- or four-story brick homes, comprised one of the oldest sections of the city, and retained much of the charm of the earlier days of the republic. Its narrow, meandering tree-lined streets and tiny alleys felt like a small town—intimate, knowable, idiosyncratic, and welcoming. The Village lay on the west side of Manhattan, and was generally understood to be bounded by 14th Street to the north, the great commercial avenue of Broadway to the east, Houston Street to the south, and the Hudson River to the west. Well served by the new subway lines, it lay between Wall Street and Midtown, and was easily reached from anywhere in New York City.

Some writers, such as Theodore Dreiser, who grew up in Terre Haute, Indiana, moved to the Village to invent new, unconventional ways of living in the world. The Hotel Albert on 10th Street became an iconic location famous for its eccentric visitors. Mark Twain, Anaïs Nin, Thomas Wolfe, and Isadora Duncan all stayed there, as did John Reed, the Communist writer who first developed his politics in the Village, then in Mexico, and finally in Russia (and was later played by Warren Beatty in the celebrated 1981 film *Reds*). In March 1911, Reed took a third-floor room in an old rooming house on the south side of Washington Square and wrote this:

Yet we are free who live in Washington Square,
We dare to think as Uptown wouldn't dare,
Blazing our nights with arguments uproarious;
What care we for a dull old world censorious,
When each is sure he'll fashion something glorious?

In 1912, the Heterodoxy Club, a feminist organization, formed in Greenwich Village with the radical idea that women should be given exactly the same freedoms as men. Many men in the Village were uncomfortable with the extent of women's freedom. Anarchist journalist Hutchins Hapgood believed that his wife was his property (probably more than half of the men in the country felt the same way about their wives) and wrote that he felt victimized because his "property" had been taken from him.

Carl Jung, the Swiss psychoanalyst, made two trips to New York, in 1912 and 1913. Beatrice Hinkle, a member of the Heterodoxy Club, introduced Jung in 1913 at a dinner party given in a three-story brick house on Patchin Place, located off 10th Street in the Village. Hinkle became the first Jungian psychoanalyst in the United States. Patchin Place still exists and houses the offices of many psychotherapists. The night Jung was there, one of the women's husbands broke the ice by starting his speech addressing a pet dog who was misbehaving with his leg: "Come, come, be reasonable, I'm not female."

In 1913, Mabel Dodge, a patron of the arts born to a wealthy banker in Buffalo, New York, bought an apartment at 23 Fifth Avenue, painted it all white, and started a salon that quickly attracted bohemian friends. Dodge, who in her younger years had been actively bisexual, was widowed from her first husband at twenty-three and estranged from her current husband, Edwin Dodge, a wealthy architect. In the Village she began an affair with John Reed and later described their first meeting: "His olive-green eyes glowed softly, his high forehead was like a baby with light brown curls rolling away from it and two spots of shining light on his temples, making him lovable. His chin was the best . . . the real poet's jawbone . . . eyebrows always lifted . . . generally breathless." Her salon solidified the Village as a magnetic attraction. As Walter Lippmann, a New York native, political commentator, and one of the founders of *The New Republic*, put it, the Village was "guided by a quality of feeling."

On a January night in 1917, six artists ventured to the Village, climbed the spiral staircase that led to the roof of the Washington Square Arch, and shot off cap pistols to declare Greenwich Village to be a "Free and Independent Republic."

Also that year, Emma Goldman, born in Russia and by then a well-known writer and speaker on women's rights in the Village, was sentenced to two years in jail for conspiring to "induce persons not to register" for the newly installed draft. Her lover, Alexander Berkman, was also sentenced. After their release from prison, they were arrested again—along with about 245 others—and boarded a boat, dubbed "the Soviet ark" by the newspapers, on

December 21, 1919, to take them to Russia. One young member of the Justice Department—twenty-five-year-old J. Edgar Hoover—wrote a congratulatory message to his superiors concerning their arrest and deportation: "Emma Goldman and Alexander Berkman are beyond a doubt the most dangerous anarchists in the country." Hoover, a special assistant to the attorney general, was one of the people who had watched the boat take off. Hoover would later take an interest in the doings of Eleanor Roosevelt.

As John Strausbaugh noted in his 2013 book *The Village: 400 Years of Beats and Bohemians, Radicals and Rogues: A History of Greenwich Village*, when the Volstead Act legalizing Prohibition went into effect in January 1920, New Yorkers went on a "liquor stampede." Liquor stores ran ads saying things like "Protect Against the Dry Days." While most of New York City pretended to obey the ban against drinking liquor, many in the Village were openly defiant. Greenwich Village had always been a wet neighborhood. It had more than fifty Irish corner saloons, whose keepers made their own wine. Every Italian-owned business in the neighborhood sold wine. Even with the advent of Prohibition, Villagers found ways to brew, ferment, and distill their own liquor and did not go dry. The library in the Village stocked books on how to set up and operate stills, and in the first six months of 1920, the number of such illegal operations increased a thousandfold in Greenwich Village.

John Sloan, a staff member of *The Masses*, a radical magazine in the Village, commented that there was a saloon on every corner in the Village in the 1910s, but by 1920 there were ten speakeasies, the saloon's clandestine substitute, on every block. Women had generally not been welcome in saloons, but the speakeasies invited both men and women, and for the first time they drank together outside of their own homes.

Looking back on the era, Police Commissioner Graven Whaler told *The New York Times*, "It didn't take more than a bottle and two chairs to make a speakeasy." Some of the speakeasies were dark hole-in-the-wall dives; others, such as the Red Head (which later moved uptown and became the 21 Club), were classier cabarets or nightclubs. In time, a number of Village tearooms, taverns, and speakeasies would cater to a gay and lesbian clientele. There were a variety of speakeasy drinks in the 1920s, with names like "Bee's Knees" and "bathtub gin," and the Ziegfeld Follies, an elaborate theatrical review of the period, opened with a funeral procession for alcohol featuring dancers with large whiskey bottles in hand and ended with an Irving Berlin song entitled "You Cannot Make Your Shimmy Shake on Tea."

In his book *Last Call: The Rise and Fall of Prohibition*, Daniel Okrent describes how writers in New York dealt with Prohibition. Willa Cather, who lived in the Village, did not abstain from liquor, though she tended to avoid it. However, when she gave parties she would fill her aquarium with gin for her guests. In her book *A Lost Lady*, Cather's heroine offers "a glittering tray" of cocktails that was "the signal for general conversation."

It was F. Scott Fitzgerald, well known to have enjoyed his liquor, who most celebrated the wet cause. In his 1922 novel *The Beautiful and Damned*, Fitzgerald presents his heroine, Gloria Patch, as a woman who "drinks excessively, drives recklessly" and "declares brazenly, 'I detest reformers, especially the sort who try to reform me.'"

Rebellious young women of the era were often referred to as "flappers," and Fitzgerald credited his wife, Zelda, for having "started the flapper movement in this country." To keep the energy moving, Fitzgerald and Zelda plunged into fountains in front of the Plaza Hotel and into the fountain in Washington Square in the Village. Zelda and other flappers smoked and drank alcohol in public and danced at jazz clubs. They also practiced sexual freedoms that shocked the Victorian morality of their parents. Zelda and Scott embraced all that was "new" and "nonconformist." Flappers also abided by the ideas of Margaret Sanger, who opened the first birth control center in the United States in Brooklyn in 1916. "Never be ashamed of passion," Sanger told young women. "If you are strongly sexed, you are richly endowed."

Eleanor, who did not drink, nor would have described herself as "strongly sexed," was not yet familiar with the ins and outs of the Village, but she was about to find her way there, on her own path to authenticity.

CHAPTER 8

Eleanor in Greenwich Village

The giving of love is an education in itself.
—*Eleanor Roosevelt*

I t was in Greenwich Village that Eleanor became the strong woman that we now know. From 1920 until the end of her life in 1962, she was actively connected to the political and social mix of the neighborhood. Paradoxically, her early years in the Village helped her gain the strength in her political convictions and in her personal confidence that would be essential to lifting Franklin to the presidency, even as their increasingly difficult marriage drove her to seek friendship and stimulation elsewhere—particularly in the Village. One might even legitimately wonder if FDR ever would have become president were it not for Eleanor's ongoing and transformative experiences in the Village.

Eleanor experienced in 1920 what Ross Wetzsteon, editor of *The Village Voice*, captured in *Republic of Dreams*: "The essence of the Village was to create a miniature society where personal idiosyncrasy could flourish through communal society. . . . Even Americans who remain hostile to the Village have become fascinated by it because it has become a kind of laboratory in which a nation at once dedicated to militant individualism and middle class conformity could witness attempts to overcome that paradox."

In 1921 Eleanor made two friends who would influence the rest of her life: Esther Everett Lape and Elizabeth Fisher Read, a lesbian couple who lived in the Village. Read was a lawyer who later became Eleanor's financial adviser, and Lape was a highly respected professor of English and journalist, and was a cofounder of the nonpartisan League of Women Voters (est. 1919). Together, they formed a three-way friendship that became the nucleus of Eleanor's support network. In the early 1920s they joined what was then called the "New Woman Movement" in Greenwich Village, part of a larger awakening and activism of educated and increasingly independent-minded women in Britain, Europe, and the U.S. that dated back to the mid-1890s. The movement organized for social change, unions for workers, equal pay for equal work, and protection for child workers, and insisted on women having their own sexual freedom. Members disagreed about politics and political parties. Some, like Eleanor, were Democrats, while others were Socialists and Communists, even Republicans.

Eleanor's brand of feminism, shaped by these women, was moved by compassion, bottled-up sexuality, and the quest for her own truth. This all happened as the Village was coming alive, working around Prohibition and freeing women to drink or smoke in public with men. There was a determination to end misunderstanding and inequality between the sexes, and Eleanor and her friends, particularly Lape and Read, laid the groundwork for tackling gender inequality that would inspire the later twentieth-century feminist movement.

Eleanor fought for women to be educated, to own their own property, and to receive equal pay for equal work. She and her friends often called themselves "the newest" of the "New Women." Unlike the younger flappers, who favored bobbed hairstyles and short skirts and frequented speakeasies, the New Women organized for social change and freely disagreed among themselves about politics and political parties. "If women could *believe* they were free," Eleanor said, "they could *behave* as if they were *free*, then they would be free."

When Eleanor was tired at the end of a weary and ragged day, she would often go to 20 East 11th Street, where Esther and Elizabeth lived. The brownstone was built in the prewar style; it was five stories tall and contained nine apartments. The street outside their house was serene, and the mood in their book-lined living room was set by beautiful rugs and objects, and for Eleanor, a feeling of comfort and of being appreciated. In the 1930s, Eleanor would rent a pied-à-terre of her own on the fourth floor, above Lape and Read. Her apartment would be small compared to her other homes, only 1,350 square feet, but it had high ceilings, good light, and a sunporch that overlooked the gardens on the roof. Eleanor often slept on the sunporch. Today, a plaque outside the house memorializes Eleanor's time in the apartment; no mention is made of Lape and Read's residence there.

As the twenties got under way, Eleanor had little interest in her appearance, but fashion was very important to Lape and Read, whose clothes were custom-made. Lape's were particularly extravagant—silks, velvets, brocades that lasted many years. Read wore dark tailored suits with string ties. In time, Eleanor used the same designer for her wardrobe. Dress is a way of expressing one's self but can also be a way of hiding. In those early years in Greenwich Village, Eleanor took her signals from the way that Lape dressed. They both wore large hats and black dresses that swept close to their ankles. Their bodies were hidden, but Eleanor held her head high, as proud of her height as she had been in England with Marie Souvestre and her circle of women friends.

The three women hosted small salons in the Greenwich Village apartment and invited other New Woman neighbors over for formal dinners. They read the classics and poetry aloud in French to one another long into the evening. The food was excellent, and even Eleanor sometimes sipped champagne. They talked about politics and organized ways that the New Women could promote rights for all women and all races of women. Many of Eleanor's

1 Eleanor (back row, center) with her classmates at Marie Souvestre's Allenswood Boarding Academy in Wimbledon, England, around 1900.

2 Franklin Delano Roosevelt, shown here at age 22 at Hyde Park, New York, in the winter of 1904. He and Eleanor were secretly engaged for a year following Franklin's proposal in the summer of 1903.

3 The omnipresent matriarch, Franklin's mother, Sara Delano Roosevelt, in 1905.

Eleanor, Franklin, and their five children (from left to right): Anna, Franklin Jr., Elliot, James, and John, photographed with Sara Roosevelt in 1919.

When Eleanor discovered Franklin's affair with her onetime social secretary Lucy Mercer, pictured here, she and FDR redefined the terms of their marriage, allowing each of them independence—political and personal—rather than divorcing.

Reporter and Communist activist John Reed was a dashing figure in the Village's bohemian circles in the prewar years.

6

Wealthy heiress and patron of the arts Mabel Dodge presided over a celebrated salon in her apartment at 23 Fifth Avenue, where she entertained the Village's artistic and political movers and shakers.

7

Mabel Dodge's living room, where she hosted her salon, featured white walls and an eclectic mélange of decor.

8

9

10

Eleanor's "New Woman" friends and political mentors, Elizabeth Read (above) and her partner, Esther Lape (center). Eleanor often took refuge in their brownstone apartment at 20 East 11th Street. In the 1930s she rented an apartment above theirs, on the fourth floor.

11

12

Eleanor with Village friends and eventual Val-Kill cohabitants
Marion Dickerman (center) and Nancy Cook (right), photographed
at Campobello in 1926. Franklin sometimes jokingly referred to
them as "she-males."

13

A summer picnic in the relaxed, easy setting of Val-Kill in 1926
with Franklin (left), Nancy Cook (center, behind ER), Eleanor
(seated on the ground), and other visiting friends.

14

Eleanor with Franklin, then governor of New York, and Marguerite "Missy" LeHand in 1929. Missy served as Franklin's personal secretary and closest confidant for more than twenty years, functioning in many ways as his second wife. During FDR's presidency, Missy acted, in effect (though unofficially), as the White House chief of staff—the first woman in that position.

A tough-talking journalist for the Associated Press, Lorena "Hick" Hickok reported on Eleanor during FDR's 1932 presidential campaign. The two women formed an intimate relationship that lasted for many years.

16

Franklin at the helm of *Amberjack II* in June 1933 following his first hundred days in office. He was determined to keep his polio-ravaged legs from public view.

17

Eleanor at Chazy Lake, New York, in 1934 with Earl Miller, her handsome driver and bodyguard, who was fiercely loyal to her, as she was to him.

A view across Washington Square Park of 29 Washington Square West (far right), the building where Eleanor and Franklin signed a lease on a penthouse apartment in 1942. After Franklin's death, Eleanor lived in this apartment at the heart of Greenwich Village until 1949.

18

Eleanor with Edith Spurlock Sampson, a lawyer and judge who was the first black U.S. delegate to the United Nations, in 1950.

19

Eleanor smiling in a photograph taken during a visit to Topeka, Kansas, three years before her death in 1962 in New York City.

20

later ideas came from these dinners. In the presence of her friends, she felt an awakening in herself and a calming of her spirit.

Elizabeth Read wrote a letter to Narcissa Cox Vanderlip about whether the cause of women's rights was more important than private relationships. The letter said in part: "If a person is lucky enough to meet a human being that is worth devotion, that—in the absence of a crisis, or an all-compelling call—is the important thing—always remembering that *selfish* devotion defeats its purpose, that limiting life to the devotion eventually kills it. In other words, it is a matter of a balance that changes every day." Eleanor remembered Read's words and put them into action—to avoid selfish ideas, to care for her own soul, to help those in need.

Eleanor also took to heart Virginia Woolf's idea that because the reality of life often overwhelms women, they must be stronger. As Woolf famously wrote: "So when I ask you to earn money and have a room of your own, I am asking you to live in the presence of reality, an invigorating life, it would appear, whether one can impart it or not." All of this Eleanor decided was necessary and in the long run she lived by Woolf's ideas: to live in the presence of what is the truth, what is strong, what is real.

The Village was a refuge for Eleanor, not just a place but an idea—the idea of following the rhythm of who she really was. In addition to spending time with Lape and Read, she also relied on another lesbian couple, Marion

Dickerman and Nancy Cook, who lived in a cooperative building at 171 West 12th Street. The poet Edna St. Vincent Millay lived at 75½ Bedford Street, which, at nine feet six inches wide, was well known as the narrowest house in the city. In 1923, Millay became the third woman to receive the Pulitzer Prize for poetry, and also joined the ranks of the New Women and declared herself a believer in free love, which made her at home in the Village. These friendships enriched and changed Eleanor's life.

In April 1921, Eleanor attended the National League's convention in Cleveland, Ohio, and was exhilarated to meet Carrie Chapman Catt, the white-haired leader of the suffrage struggle, who spoke in support of the League of Nations and said: "Men were born by instinct to slay. It seems God is giving a call to the women of the world to come forward, to stay the hand of men, to say: 'No, you should no longer kill your fellow men.'"

Even though she had her own ideas and interests, Eleanor knew she would also have to focus on her husband's work, and expressed enthusiasm for doing so. In a note to Franklin from the convention in Cleveland, she wrote: "I've had a very interesting day and heard some really good women speakers. Mrs. Catt has clear cold reason. . . . Minnie Fisher Cunningham from Texas is emotional and idealistic, but she made everyone cry!" Eleanor finished her note to Franklin this way: "Much, much love dear and I prefer to do my politics with you."

In the spring of 1922, Nancy Cook, serving as the head

of the Women's Division of the New York Democratic Party, telephoned Eleanor and asked her to be a speaker for a fund-raising luncheon for activist women Democrats. Eleanor hesitated. She was a reluctant public speaker at the time. Her voice went up several octaves when speaking, which then made her giggle uncontrollably. She later tamed the monster, with Louis Howe's help, and in time became a very good public speaker. But Howe encouraged Eleanor to speak at the luncheon. Eleanor arrived at the luncheon with a bouquet of violets for Nancy Cook. As Blanche Wiesen Cook explained in her biography, "Between women, gifts of violets were quite the rage during the 1920s—they appear again and again in feminist literature as an international symbol of affection." From then on, Eleanor considered Nancy Cook a close friend and called her Nan. A potter, photographer, and carpenter, Nan had short, wiry hair and an intense personality. She and her partner, Marion Dickerman, had met in graduate school at Syracuse University and had become lovers not long after. Marion was tall, ladylike, and quieter than Nan. In 1917, during the First World War, both Nan and Marion went to London as volunteers for the Red Cross. Marion quickly took to nursing the many wounded men, but Nan, a gifted craftsperson, used her skills to make artificial limbs for soldiers.

Of the two women, Eleanor favored Nan, whom she called a "boyish" girl. Both Eleanor and Nan were experienced political organizers, but Nan was also funny and roguish, and with her, Eleanor did things that horrified her mother-in-law, who particularly disapproved of Nan's masculine clothes. Eleanor once appeared with Nan at a family event, dressed in matching knickerbocker outfits with vest and jacket. To his credit, Franklin welcomed Nan and Marion to his and Eleanor's circle of close friends. Often he teased the women; he was "Uncle Franklin" and they were "the girls." Louis Howe and Franklin joked that the women were "she-males," a loaded phrase that conveyed their belief that Eleanor and her women friends would never be equal to men at home or in politics. Nancy and Marion laughed at FDR's joke, but Eleanor was not amused. Nor was she likely pleased when her cousin Alice called Nancy and Marion "female impersonators."

Eleanor was increasingly caught between two lives: the life she had once had with Franklin versus the life she now had in the Village with other New Women. In June 1921, Eleanor asked Lape and Read, who were open about their lesbian relationship, to stay for a few days at Hyde Park with her and her family. "My mother-in-law was distressed," wrote Eleanor. "I had begun to realize that in my development I was drifting far afield from the old influences."

At the end of their stay, Lape remembered, "Franklin took us to the station, carrying our bags. He was wearing one of those baggy brown suits. He looked so strong and healthy." That would be the last time that Esther saw Franklin standing on his own two feet.

CHAPTER 9

Polio Strikes

I know that he had real fear when he was first taken ill.
—*Eleanor Roosevelt*

In July 1921, Eleanor and her children arrived on Campobello, an island with dramatic tides and beautiful sunsets, located in New Brunswick, Canada, close to Maine, where the family always spent their summer holiday. Franklin had business in New York but expected to leave on Friday, August 5, and make the four-day trip up the coast to Campobello with Van Lear Black, a wealthy New York businessman, on the USS *Sabalo*, which Black had newly purchased for use as his private yacht.

Normally Franklin felt calm on sea voyages, but that day the *Sabalo* came across a deep fog off the coast of Maine. Franklin knew the tides well and took the helm. He navigated blindly by following the sounds of the foghorns. However, while passing bait and hooks to fellow travelers, Franklin slipped and fell overboard. Normally the cold waters did not bother him, but this time he was shaken by the chill. "I'd never felt anything so cold as that water," he said later. "I hardly wet my head because I still had hold of the tender, but the water was so cold it seemed paralyzing."

The following day, August 10, FDR complained of a headache and seemed tired, but he took his three older children, Anna, Elliott, and James, for a sail in the Bay of Fundy on board the twenty-four-foot keel sloop *Vireo*. In the distance, Franklin saw a forest fire and went ashore with his children to beat out the flames with pine boughs. "Later in the afternoon we brought it under control," Franklin wrote. "Our eyes were bleary with smoke; we were be-grimed, smarting with spark burns, exhausted." In an effort to shake his exhaustion, FDR took a short dip in the Bay's cold waters to revive himself, but said he did not feel the "glow I expected." When he returned to the house, Franklin looked over his mail in his wet bathing suit. At the dinner table, he complained of aches and chills and went to bed.

FDR did not yet know it, but his reaction to the cold water that day, as when he fell overboard the *Sabalo*, was an early warning symptom of poliomyelitis, known then as "infantile paralysis." Hugh Gregory Gallagher, a historian who contracted polio at the age of nineteen and was encased in an iron lung for many months, wrote in *FDR's Splendid Deception* that on that day in the water, Roosevelt's central nervous system was under attack from the polio virus, which explained his heightened sensitivity to changes of light, temperature, and pressure upon his skin. "The chill was a warning," wrote Gallagher, "but it was a warning he did not heed."

The next morning FDR felt worse. His left leg dragged, and within a few hours he could not move it at all. When his daughter, Anna, brought a tray to his bedroom, Franklin managed to show her a weak smile. By then, his temperature was at 102 degrees. Eleanor sent for Dr. Eben Bennet, who lived in the town of Lubec, Maine, not far from Campobello. Bennet arrived, checked Franklin's fever, and told Eleanor it might be a cold or the flu. By Saturday, Franklin was paralyzed from his chest down, and his skin and muscles were so sensitive that he could not bear the touch of bedclothes on his skin.

In 1921, Franklin was at the prime of a demanding political life, having won election to the New York State Senate in 1910 and been named assistant secretary of the navy under President Woodrow Wilson. In the presidential election of 1920, Roosevelt had been the vice-presidential running mate of the Democrats' nominee, James M. Cox of Ohio. Though Cox lost the race for the presidency, Franklin had established himself as a strong Democratic leader. During the 1920 convention in San Francisco, Franklin, a young champion with a flashing smile, had rallied the discouraged Democrats. One year later, he was an invalid at age thirty-nine.

For two weeks, Eleanor slept on the couch in Franklin's room and took care of him as he lay helpless in the bed. He and his wife had not been physically intimate for several years, but nonetheless it was Eleanor who stayed by his side, turning him from side to side on the bed and calling for Louis Howe when she needed help to lift him. By then almost all the muscles from FDR's chest down were no longer functioning. In addition, there was no strength in his thumbs—he could not hold a pen. Imagine FDR locked in his bed, having to be positioned on a bedpan by Eleanor, who also routinely inserted a rubber catheter through the urethra of his penis and into his bladder.

What are we to make of the way Franklin and Eleanor handled the early days of his polio? Eleanor called it a "trial by fire," a statement that Franklin later used in speeches. Part of the reason may have been that they were born during the Victorian Age and were not the least bit demonstrative; they kept their feelings to themselves. From the moment that Franklin lost the use of his body, they had a new bond. Eleanor and Louis Howe put their hearts and souls into caring for him. Eleanor became his nurse and Franklin was her patient. The romance in their marriage had ended long ago, but the pursuit of Franklin's political life and Eleanor's interest in politics were just beginning.

On August 25, Dr. Robert R. Lovett, a specialist in poliomyelitis from Boston, came to Campobello. As Joseph Lash recounts in *Eleanor and Franklin,* when Lovett arrived, he examined Franklin and made his diagnosis: infantile paralysis. When Eleanor heard the diagnosis, she immediately thought of the six children in the house, her own five children and Hartley Howe, the son of Louis Howe, who were much more likely than adults to contract the disease. She had allowed their children to come to the door of FDR's sickroom once a day and instructed them to be quiet. She didn't have the courage to tell them that Franklin had polio, but they all knew he was very ill. Elliott thought his father might have had a heart attack. Dr. Lovett told Eleanor that if the children were going to be stricken with polio, it would have already happened and assured her it was likely they had not been infected.

When Sara Delano Roosevelt's ship returning her from a trip to Europe pulled in to New York harbor on Tuesday, August 30, she was surprised that Franklin was not on the dock to welcome her home. Her brother, Fred, and sister, Kassie, were there instead. Fred handed her a letter from Eleanor explaining that Franklin had been "quite ill" and that she, Franklin, and the children would be happy to see her. Fred was left to tell Sara the details of FDR's malady. The next day, Sara left New York on a train north to Eastport, Maine, and rode on a motorboat across the bay to Campobello.

Franklin and Eleanor were ready for her. Sara wrote later that she found him a "brave, smiling and beautiful son." Franklin joked to her that he was glad she was back and that he had "got up this party for you!" He smiled from ear to ear. Sara noticed that below his waist he did not move at all. "His legs (that I have always been proud of) have to be moved as they ache when long in position," she told Fred. "He and Eleanor decided to be cheerful and the atmosphere of the house is all happiness, so I have fallen in and follow their glorious example."

Sara stayed for a few days, but it was clear to her that it was difficult for Franklin to pretend to be happy. There was little for her to do on Campobello as Eleanor was providing most of Franklin's care, so she returned to New York.

After four weeks, Howe had worked out a plan to move FDR from Campobello to Presbyterian Hospital, located on 70th Street and Madison Avenue in New York. While still on Campobello, Howe had misled reporters about FDR's condition. He told them that Franklin had a heavy cold, then he told them it was influenza, from which he was "not improving." Finally, the story became that Franklin had a "mild" case of polio.

On Tuesday, September 13, Howe had FDR strapped to a canvas-type stretcher that was then passed out of the house and down the cliff by six men from the island. Franklin, in pain the entire time, especially when the stretcher was jostled, was carried onto a small boat, which took him two miles across the sea to a sardine dock. There, the stretcher was rolled on a baggage cart to a private railroad car, where a window was removed so that the stretcher could be passed through to a waiting berth.

Eleanor had their dog, Duffy, a Scottish terrier, in her lap, and Franklin lay in the berth on the window side and smoked with his favorite cigarette holder. As the *New York World* reported the next day, "Mr. Roosevelt was enjoying his cigarette and said he had a good appetite." It was not that simple. FDR had experienced several days of pain throughout his body. He and Eleanor had to face two more days on the train while Franklin wrestled with his agonizing discomfort. In spite of the pain, Franklin did not show fear, smoking his cigarette and displaying his famous smile as he passed through one station after another. He considered it the first public test of his resolve to beat the disease, but Eleanor was frightened and exhausted.

On September 15, a handful of reporters were waiting at Grand Central Terminal in New York. Howe told them that Roosevelt had had a "comfortable trip" and was "feeling very well." On the following day, the story made the front page of *The New York Times*, which for the first time reported that FDR was suffering from poliomyelitis. He was seen by Dr. George Draper, an orthopedic specialist and a friend of Franklin's from Harvard, who was not a polio expert. He explained that Roosevelt's "attack was very mild," however he was still unable to walk. "I cannot say how long Mr. Roosevelt will be kept in the hospital," said Dr. Draper to the press, "but you can say definitely that he will not be crippled." Eleanor assumed that he would gradually improve, and she was relieved on hearing that he would "definitely" not be crippled.

But after watching FDR for the first week, Draper changed his mind. FDR's recovery was very slow, and the muscle masses on either side of his spine were falling away. "The lower extremities present a most depressing picture."

His chart read: "Not improving." Franklin was discharged from the hospital at the end of October but kept in touch with Draper, who became a lifelong friend. He was taken to his mother's home at 47-49 East 65th Street, and carried to his upstairs bedroom. Howe lived with him during the week, and there were full-time nurses to dress him and help him in the bathroom.

When Eleanor was at the house, she slept in one of the boys' rooms. Eleanor became his stand-in with Democratic leaders, especially those in New York, and kept his name before the public. She wrestled with the question of how to keep FDR viable as a candidate in future elections. She was aware that no "crippled" man had ever become the president of the United States, a goal that she was not ready to abandon for FDR. To keep him surrounded by politicians, she brought some of his friends, including his navy boss, Josephus Daniels, to Sara's house, which helped FDR feel at ease. In return, the friends talked politics with Franklin and kept him up to date.

Eleanor's biggest problem was Sara. All through the winter of 1922, a battle raged between them. Sara insisted that public life was for healthy men, and that Franklin must let go of his dreams and retire to Hyde Park. Sara had spent years tending her invalid husband, James, until his death, and thought she should now do the same for Franklin. Eleanor believed the only thing Sara offered was pity for Franklin and that she treated him like an invalid, despite the fact he clearly wished to be treated otherwise.

In *This Is My Story*, Eleanor described the conflict that seethed that winter: "My mother-in-law thought we were tiring my husband and that he should be kept completely quiet, which made the discussions as to his care somewhat acrimonious on occasion. . . . She had made up her mind that Franklin was going to be an invalid for the rest of his life and that he would retire to Hyde Park and live there."

Eleanor wanted more time with FDR and with her pursuits in the Village. But there were unanswerable questions. Would FDR ever be able to walk? Would he be able to stand? Would he be seen everywhere as an invalid? Could a paralyzed man run for political office? It had never happened before. Franklin could not stand without braces or walk without assistance, but he was still vigorous and appeared young. When he saw people, he did his best to stand erect, flash his big smile, laugh heartily, and insist he would soon be back on his feet. He believed that he would walk soon, and because he believed it Eleanor pretended to believe it, too.

When asked if he wanted to talk about it, Franklin usually said no. He would not allow negative talk about his illness. However, on one occasion in 1921, Franklin had a bad day and met with Beatrice Hinkle, the Jungian psychologist, to discuss how he could deal with the onset of dark depression. Hinkle knew Eleanor through their membership in Chi Omega, a society of professional women. It was Eleanor who asked Hinkle to help Franklin lift up his spirits as he dealt with his paralysis.

Both Eleanor and Louis Howe supported and cared for Franklin from the beginning of his illness. Both wanted to see him back in politics, if possible.

In the end, Eleanor and Louis won their battle, since FDR eventually returned to public life, but, as Hugh Gregory Gallagher explained, Franklin's mother prevailed as well. For several years, Franklin shifted his focus between politics and recovery from his paralysis. Sara was delighted he spent much of each year at Hyde Park. He began swimming three times a week in his friend William Astor's pool and pond, not too far from his mother's home. He realized that the water supported his legs with ease and used swimming as his main exercise. It was a comfort for Eleanor to know that Franklin was rehabilitating his legs.

In January 1922, FDR was fitted for braces that locked at the knee and extended along the length of his leg, and by the spring he could stand with assistance. He decided that one day he would walk the length of his driveway at Hyde Park. LeRoy Jones, his African American valet, helped Franklin into his braces, wheeled him out to the front of the house, and handed him his crutches. The driveway was half a mile long, with trees on either side. Each day Franklin lunged forward on his crutches, dragging his feet after him, hoping that he would eventually be able to walk. He often fell to the ground, but LeRoy lifted him up and helped put him into his wheelchair. FDR's mission was to make it to the end of the driveway. He never once made it to the end, but he never stopped trying.

CHAPTER 10

Franklin and Eleanor, the Years Apart

A woman is like a tea bag, you never know
how strong it is until it's in hot water.
—*Eleanor Roosevelt*

There were few times in Eleanor Roosevelt's life when she broke down and cried, but one afternoon in April 1922, in the house on 65th Street, a cloud loomed over her life. Eleanor was reading aloud to her youngest boys, six-year-old Johnnie and seven-year-old Franklin Jr., but she felt so overwhelmed that she sobbed and could not stop. "Elliott came in from school, dashed in to look at me and fled. Mr. Howe came in and tried to find out what was the matter with me, but he gave it up as a bad job," she later wrote. Nothing relieved her distress. She finally went over to her mother-in-law's side of the house, found an empty room, and "locked the door and poured cold water on a towel and mopped my face. Eventually I pulled myself together."

Eleanor had good reason to cry. Though she believed

that Franklin's strength and courage would help him find the patience to endure whatever lay ahead, she worried about their children. Playing games with them had been Franklin's role. Life without him, while he was away at Hyde Park ill with polio, was difficult for them. She decided that if her children were "going to have a normal existence without a father to do these things with them, I would have to become a good deal more companionable and more of an all-around person than I had ever been before."

Eleanor pitched in with her boys; she took them swimming, sailing, hiking, and at night they all made camp to watch the stars. She bought herself a car to take them places. She in effect became mother and father to the children, especially during the early months of Franklin's illness.

Her fifteen-year-old daughter, Anna, did not want to play with the boys. Instead, Eleanor enrolled her in New York's Miss Chapin's School with the hope that the school would be as welcoming as Eleanor's school with Mademoiselle Souvestre had been. Anna was tall and beautiful but complex. She felt rejected at Miss Chapin's School and equally rejected at home. As the only girl in the family, Anna was not interested in her mother's opinions because she loved her father first. In a way, Eleanor had done the same thing when she was young. Anna knew that her father had come close to death from his illness and stayed close by his side.

To her credit, Anna went to her mother to ask directly why Eleanor did not love her. Perhaps Anna thought

Eleanor was too busy, or had other things on her mind. In any regard, she assured Anna that she was wrong and that she did love her. Then Eleanor poured out her troubles and explained about Franklin's love affair with Lucy Mercer, explaining that this was why she and Franklin no longer shared the same bed. Eleanor told Anna that she regretted that she had not been close enough to her children and asked Anna to forgive her. Afterward, Anna could understand more of her mother's pain. The two grew closer, attending political events and the theater together.

The children knew that their father's life would never be the same after the attack of polio. Day by day, Eleanor encouraged FDR to continue his treatments and urged him to stay focused on his career in politics. In one of her journals, Eleanor wrote that the polio crisis "gave him strength and courage he had not had before. He had to think out the fundamentals of living and learn the greatest of all lessons—infinite patience and never-ending persistence." Eleanor believed that polio would make him a better man. But would it make her a better woman? Like many women, Eleanor did not yet have the easy ability to stand up for herself. At some point she began to understand that hers was now a "political marriage" and not a traditional one. Given these circumstances, she decided she would do something useful by becoming Franklin's "eyes and ears" and helping open a path to a political career for Franklin and later for herself.

After 1923 Franklin and Eleanor were often not together. Their relationship moved from a traditional marriage to a professional collaboration between equals. Eleanor was free to engage with political women in Greenwich Village, while Franklin worked hard with Louis Howe to figure out how he could run for political office as a partially paralyzed man. He also needed to find intimacy with a woman who was not Eleanor, for in February 1920 Lucy Mercer had married Winthrop Rutherfurd, a wealthy widower who as a young socialite had once courted the heiress Consuelo Vanderbilt.

Franklin found what he needed with his secretary, Marguerite LeHand, nicknamed "Missy" by FDR's sons. FDR's sons liked Missy a great deal. She had been born into a blue-collar Irish-American family, was five feet seven, had dark eyes and a broad smile. Missy would serve as FDR's secretary for twenty-one years. In February 1923, Franklin and Missy spent six weeks on a rented houseboat, the *Larooco*, cruising off the coast of Florida. LeRoy (who had also been aboard) lifted him on and off the boat and carried him from place to place. On the boat, FDR could remove the heavy steel corset and braces that went from his hips to his shoes. Franklin was convinced the warm sea helped his muscles and circulation. In the waters off the boat, he was free to swim. Nonetheless, it had been a year and a half since he had contracted polio. His doctors saw no way that he would ever walk again as a healthy man. There were many days that he pulled himself out of his depression in order to greet the numerous guests on the *Larooco*.

Eleanor invited her friend Esther Lape along on one of these boat trips, though the two of them stayed for only one week. Howe was there as well, and worried that Franklin might spend the rest of his life on the boat, entertaining friends. If Franklin wanted to get back into politics, Howe told him he had to be seen upright, on crutches. Eleanor agreed. The aimless days at sea drove her crazy and she dreaded every minute of the trip. "When we anchored at night and the wind blew, it all seemed eerie and menacing to me," she recalled. "The beauty of the moon and the stars only added to the strangeness of the dark waters and the tropic vegetation, and on occasion it could be colder and more uncomfortable than tales of the sunny South led me to believe was possible." Lape wrote a letter in March 1923 to a mutual friend, saying, "I was happy to be with Eleanor Roosevelt when there was nothing for either of us to do. She is an utterly splendid person."

The question of whether Missy and FDR's relationship was sexual has been debated by a long string of historians. Hazel Rowley believes that "there is no doubt that Franklin's relationship with Missy was romantic," but whether sex was possible is unknown, due to FDR's disability. Still, a man as astute as Franklin might have figured out his own way. Doris Kearns Goodwin writes that "beneath the complexity . . . it is absolutely clear that Franklin was the love of Missy's life, and he adored her and depended on her for affection and support as well as work." Blanche Wiesen Cook described Eleanor as treating Missy warmly, "as an elder daughter or, in the manner of Asian matriarchs, as the junior wife."

FDR's second-oldest son, Elliott, in his book *An Untold Story: The Roosevelts of Hyde Park* described often seeing Missy sitting on his father's lap and claims that "she shared a familiar life in all its aspects with father." Elliott's older brother, James "Jimmy" Roosevelt II, was writing a book about his father, later published as *My Parents, a Differing View* (1976), and did not believe that his father and Missy engaged in sex. "I suppose you could say they came to love one another," Jimmy wrote, "but it was not a physical love." Hugh Gregory Gallagher, a polio victim himself, has asserted there was likely no actual lovemaking between FDR and Missy. "In the sexual act he would be vulnerable to hurt and humiliation," writes Gallagher. "More important and more frightening is that he would be naked to himself—forced to acknowledge and confront the full extent of his loss and to cope with the fury engendered by that loss."

In the summer of 1924, Howe convinced Alfred E. Smith, the governor of New York, who was running to be the Democratic nominee for president, that FDR should give the speech to nominate Smith at the party's convention. Smith was popular in New York but was progressive, which would not sit well outside the state. In addition, he was a Catholic, and there had never been a Catholic president. Howe realized that FDR had little to lose in making the speech as long as Franklin was never photographed in his wheelchair or seen being carried. Howe concentrated on how to make people believe Franklin was strong enough to walk.

Eleanor was in favor of FDR delivering the speech, as it was a tremendous opportunity for him to restart his political life. She and Louis Howe worked through the details of how to avoid the press. They also worked with James in getting FDR safely to the podium, which was firmly anchored to allow Franklin to support himself with his two hands during his presentation.

On the morning of June 26, 1924, the crowd at Madison Square Garden grew quiet when Franklin leaned heavily on his son's arm. James handed him one crutch and then a second. Then Franklin and his son made their way slowly across the stage. In her seat in the gallery, Eleanor took out her knitting basket—knit one, purl two—and remembered that when she and Franklin were newlyweds they knitted together. That day, Eleanor knitted on her own to calm herself.

Finally, Franklin, dressed in a gray-and-white suit, reached the speaker's podium, and held fast to it as James carefully took away both crutches. Then Franklin beamed as he looked into the crowd over his small glasses and threw back his head, laughing. The crowd clapped and cheered. Franklin spoke for half an hour as the crowd applauded. The Roosevelt name carried great weight in New York City and in rural upstate New York. When Franklin finished, he saluted Al Smith as "the happy warrior of the political battlefield." Again, the crowd went bonkers.

Franklin's speech was the high point of the convention. The people were not screaming for Smith as the happy warrior; instead they stood on their feet and clapped their hands for Roosevelt, the hero who had conquered adversity against all odds by fighting polio. It all played out just as Howe had hoped. Franklin was ready to renew his plans to run for political office. The careful planning and rehearsal by Howe, Eleanor, and James allowed Franklin to steal the spotlight that night.

On October 3, 1924, Franklin, Missy, and Eleanor arrived by train at Warm Springs, Georgia. A friend of Franklin's from Harvard days, George Peabody, had written to Franklin about a local man who had polio and had improved from therapy in the thermal springs there. Tom Loyless, the manager of the springs, met them at the station. Franklin was desperate to try for a miraculous cure. Everything about Warm Springs was primitive. The cottage where Franklin and Eleanor stayed was a firetrap; there was no running water or electricity, and the kitchen was unusable and almost uninhabitable. Eleanor saw daylight pouring through the cracks in the walls. The next morning Loyless took them down the hill to an open-air pool. The mineral salts floated over the water. Franklin concluded that this pool would be his healing place. In later years, he purchased the thermal springs for himself and other polio victims.

Eleanor returned to New York, leaving Franklin and Missy to the mountainous backwoods of Georgia and the fields of cotton and tobacco. "It's too bad that Eleanor had to leave so soon," Franklin wrote to his mother, "but she and I both feel it is important for her not to be away at the end of the campaign as long as I have to be by myself."

In New York, Eleanor, coached by Howe, worked hard to organize women to vote. She was one of the few New York Democrats who stumped in rural areas and urged farmers to vote Democratic. It was in these rural areas that Eleanor discovered how much women had to learn about exercising their right to vote. "They have the vote, they have the power, but they don't seem to know what to do with it," Eleanor told Rose Feld of *The New York Times* in 1924. She understood that men were often hostile to notions of their wives voting, and she summed up their attitude toward women who ventured into politics this way: "You are wonderful. I love and honor you. . . . Lead your own lives, attend to your charities, travel when you wish, bring up the children, run your house, I'll give you all the freedom you wish and all the money I can but—leave me my business and politics." Her message to women was much more hopeful by contrast: "Get into the game and stay in it. Throwing mud from the outside won't help. Building up from the inside will." She suggested that women should attempt to "think like men," as she was beginning to do since Franklin's diagnosis with polio. In her family she had to "think like men" in order to help sustain Franklin's political ambitions.

In the end, Smith did not win the nomination for the

presidency, despite FDR's remarkable speech. Al Smith decided to run for governor of New York instead that same year, and Eleanor campaigned vigorously for him throughout the state.

In 1924, the Democratic National Committee asked Eleanor to chair its platform committee on women's issues. She agreed and sought recommendations from "all women's organizations in the country" on what the party platform should state. When the male committee refused to adopt any of the women's recommendations for the platform and forced Eleanor to sit outside the room while they deliberated, she took their rebuke to heart, recalling: "For the first time the women stood when it came to a national convention. I shortly discovered that they were of little importance. They stood outside the door of all important meetings and waited." The male decision makers were not interested in dealing with women's issues. Eleanor may have taken this rebuke to heart, but she never gave up.

In October 1924, Republicans nominated her cousin Theodore Roosevelt Jr., son of Teddy, to oppose Al Smith for governor of New York. Theodore said FDR "does not wear the brand of our family," a remark that infuriated Eleanor. Nancy Cook and Marion Dickerman drove with her in an automobile topped with a giant steaming teapot made of papier-mâché, in an attempt to associate her cousin with the Teapot Dome scandal, in which the administration of President Warren G. Harding had been implicated. The bribery scandal involved giveaways to private oil interests. In her Teapot Dome automobile Eleanor drove through small and large towns and explained that while her cousin, Theodore Jr., was a nice enough man, his public service record showed him "willing to do the bidding of his friends." Given her closeness to the late president, Eleanor's attack on Teddy Jr. did not go over well with their families, but Eleanor did not flinch.

Politics had become what she called her "choicest interest." She was now known as a competent political insider. Mainstream feminism often operated through organizations, and Eleanor was an enthusiastic joiner. Within a short period of time, as a result of her new friends in Greenwich Village, she had become an important figure in the League of Women Voters, the Women's Trade Union League, and the Women's Division of the New York State Democratic Committee. Newspapers called her for statements. In 1925, Eleanor made her radio debut, promoting the agendas of women.

Howe continued to coach Eleanor in her public speaking. She followed his suggestions and in time became an excellent public speaker. Eleanor understood that it was difficult for Franklin not to be front and center in politics, and wherever she went, she kept Franklin's name alive by making speeches and assuring friends that Franklin would soon be back in the political arena. On February 6, 1925, she wrote him a letter in response to his recent praise of her. "You need not be proud of me, dear," she wrote. "I'm only being active till you can be again—it isn't such a great desire on my part to serve the world and I'll fall back into habits of sloth quite easily! Hurry up for as you know my ever present sense of the uselessness of all things will over-whelm me sooner or later."

March 17, 1925, marked Franklin and Eleanor's twen-tieth wedding anniversary. Eleanor went on a train ride to Florida to be with Franklin. She wrote in her diary that she had long ago accepted the fact that Franklin would not offer the love that she wanted, and she grieved over it. "No form of love is to be despised," she wrote, quot-ing from *The Constant Nymph*, a 1924 novel that she was reading, about a teenage girl who falls in love with a cousin and marries him. The novel must have reminded her of her early life as the bride of Franklin, her cousin, and how happy she once was, and it suggests that she still felt some kind of love, or perhaps a better word is *commitment*, to-ward Franklin. As Eleanor later wrote, she learned "not to demand the impossible." While they talked fairly regularly and remained close companions, they made sure to allow each other an independent life. Their lives came together at Christmas, Thanksgiving, birthdays, and anniversaries. Thanksgiving was spent at Warm Springs, Christmas was celebrated at Hyde Park, and usually their anniversary was spent in Florida.

CHAPTER 11

J. Edgar Hoover
in the Village

No one can make you feel inferior without your consent.
—*Eleanor Roosevelt*

E leanor's unorthodox activities in Greenwich Village did not go unnoticed by J. Edgar Hoover, the director of the Justice Department's Bureau of Investigation (it would be renamed the Federal Bureau of Investigation in 1935), whom we last saw deporting Emma Goldman and others on "the Soviet ark." The first entry in Eleanor's massive file was logged in 1924 when Hoover ordered his agents to launch a "General Investigation" of Eleanor, Esther Lape, and Narcissa Cox Vanderlip for their support of the entrance of the United States into the World Court and the League of Nations. Few in Congress supported the idea, and both Eleanor and Lape were criticized in the press. Though her Bureau of Investigation file began over concerns about her activities in the Village, it grew to thirty-nine hundred pages in her lifetime—one of the largest files in Hoover's collection—and even today some of its reports are not open to public inspection. From Hoover's point of view Eleanor was a troublemaker who consorted with the wrong people.

Throughout the 1920s, Eleanor's support for the World Court and the League of Nations did not falter. She and Lape cochaired the American Peace Award Committee. The prize was established by Edward Bok, the former editor and publisher of *Ladies' Home Journal*, who offered a prize of $50,000 to the plan that would "provide practicable means whereby the United States can take its place and do its share toward preserving world peace." Soon a staggering 22,165 plans for peace were submitted to a jury made up of legal scholars, but most of the people in Congress thought the peace prize was a waste of time. When the Senate met to consider it, the committee room was filled by more than seven hundred men and women, who, according to *The New York Times*, cheered for Lape, the key witness.

J. Edgar Hoover had been hired by the Justice Department's Alien Enemy Bureau in 1917. At the age of twenty-four, he was entrusted by Attorney General A. Mitchell Palmer, whose house was famously bombed by anarchists in 1919, with leading the department's new Radical Division. It was this industrious young investigator who led what would become known as the Palmer Raids (1919–20) against anarchists, resulting in the deportation of Emma Goldman and Alexander Berkman, among other subversives (actual and suspected).

Hoover regarded the Bok Hearings as the work of socialists and voguish leftie women—namely Eleanor, Lape, and Vanderlip. Many congressmen agreed with Hoover, and the Bok Peace Prize was suspended by Congress. The battle was temporarily over, but Eleanor's passion for peace grew stronger. Hoover had a fear and hatred of Communism and suspected that Eleanor was soft on Communists. He also thought she was too comfortable in the company of lesbian women. As he did with others, Hoover believed he could secretly intuit Eleanor's true nature, and decided that he did not believe she was who she said she was.

On the streets of the Village Eleanor joined picket lines for the Women's Trade Union; she protested improper working conditions for garment workers and inadequate wages, and like the other women in protest marches, Eleanor was charged with disorderly conduct by the police, arrested, and sent to jail.

Hoover closely monitored people such as Barney Josephson, a Jewish man who would go on to open New York's first integrated nightclub, Café Society, at Sheridan Square in the Village in 1938. Josephson's goal with his nightclub was to find a place for progressive white people to go. By then Prohibition was over and businessmen such as Barney were legitimate, unlike the criminals who ran the nightclubs, speakeasies, and stills of that era. Café Society was frequented by Eleanor and her friends, including people such as the screenwriter and dramatist Lillian Hellman, novelist and sportswriter Budd Schulberg, and *New Yorker* writer and editor St. Clair McKelway, as well as prominent African Americans such as James Baldwin.

Eleanor's file and certain others considered "special" were kept separate from all the rest of the FBI files. They were stored not in Hoover's office, but in the office of his secretary, Miss Helen Gandy. She had begun working for Hoover in 1918, before he was appointed director, and worked for him until his death in 1972. Like Hoover she was single, and she was completely devoted to her boss. She was the only one he trusted with the secret files that included Eleanor's.

The FBI manual gave clear instructions for interviewing and investigating any suspicious person. Techniques included asking neighbors: What kind of car does she drive? Are there indications she is living above her means? Is she ever drunk? Are strange visitors coming to her home? Is she having loud parties? Does subversive-looking mail come to you by mistake? Ever seen the *Daily Worker*, a socialist newspaper? Do you have any reason to suspect that she might not be 100 percent American?

Many of Eleanor's interests and friends in Greenwich Village managed to rouse Hoover's suspicions. She believed that Hoover did not understand women's empowerment, different sexual preferences, nor the rights of African Americans. Evidence that Hoover might have been homosexual himself suggests a hypocritical fixation with Eleanor and her lesbian friends.

CHAPTER 12

Finding Her Own Way

Val-Kill is where I used to find myself and grow.
At Val-Kill I emerged as an individual.
—*Eleanor Roosevelt*

Eleanor always wanted to have a home of her own. She and Franklin had lived in houses built by her mother-in-law, Sara—the family house in Hyde Park and the two connected six-story townhouses on East 65th Street in New York. Neither of those felt like Eleanor's home. She knew that Sara did not like her defiant women friends, each of them sharing an apartment as Eleanor had done within the cooperative building at 20 East 11th Street in Greenwich Village, all activist women, many of them lesbians.

One summer evening in 1924, Eleanor, Nancy Cook, and Marion Dickerman picnicked in a favorite spot at Hyde Park, located two miles from the Springwood Estate, on the eastern side of Franklin's property, down on the banks of a stream called Val-Kill, Dutch for "Valley Stream." Eleanor remarked it would be their last picnic at Val-Kill for the season because Sara planned to close the Big House.

113

According to Marion, it was FDR who thought of building a home for Eleanor and her feminist friends at Val-Kill. "But aren't you girls silly?" wrote FDR. "This isn't Mother's land. I bought this acreage myself. And why shouldn't you three have a cottage of your own, so you could come and go as you please?"

On August 5, 1924, Franklin gave the property to Eleanor, Nancy, and Marion, and the three would share the cost of maintaining the cottage he would have built for them there. FDR wanted them to have a traditional Hudson River Dutch colonial farmhouse made of stone. He called Elliot Brown, a friend from his navy days, and asked him to serve as his contractor. "My Missus and some of her female political friends want to build a shack on a stream in the back woods and want, instead of a beautiful marble bath, to have the stream dug out so as to form an old-fashioned swimming hole."

Franklin took control of the Val-Kill construction process, which irritated Eleanor, who wanted to build her own house with her own hands. FDR worked with Henry Toombs, the architect, for the plans. The bids he received were inflated, and Eleanor worried they could not afford the house. "If you three girls will just go away and leave us alone," FDR said, "Henry and I will build the cottage." True to his word, on New Year's Day, 1926, Franklin officially opened Val-Kill Cottage to their friends and families. When he presented Val-Kill, he told the three women, "Welcome to your honeymoon cottage." This line probably was also an irritant to Eleanor. Was he just joking or implying something else?

He inscribed a book, *Little Marion's Pilgrimage*, to Marion. "To my little pilgrim, whose progress is always upward and onward, to the things of beauty and the thoughts of love, and the like—From her affectionate Uncle Franklin, on the occasion of the love nest on Val-Kill." Sara, angry about the "all-woman cottage nonsense," made a fuss, but Eleanor did not make an issue of it. The living room was full of books and newspapers. In the spring Eleanor and her friends had picnics, and in summer enjoyed swimming parties. Despite her having been irritated by the construction process and Franklin's formal presentation, Val-Kill helped transform Eleanor significantly.

Nancy and Marion immediately made Val-Kill their home. Upstairs were two bedrooms; Nancy and Marion shared one, and Eleanor had a private room, although she did not often spend the night. She went back and forth between Hyde Park and New York, where she stayed in the Village. She was determined to make her own money. Louis Howe encouraged Eleanor to start a monthly magazine, *Women's Democratic News*. In 1925 she began her own commercially sponsored radio program that was broadcast twice a week on NBC. (By the 1930s, she earned up to $3,000 for one appearance on the radio program—an amount equivalent to $50,000 in today's currency. "Isn't it a fact that women have always worked, often very hard," said Eleanor when the press complained. "Did anyone make a fuss about it until they began to be paid for their work?")

Money was on her mind. At the end of April 1925, Eleanor went to Warm Springs in Georgia to try to convince Franklin not to purchase the resort. "Don't let yourself in for too much money," Eleanor told him. When Franklin was at Warm Springs, he and Missy often had the place to themselves. Each morning Franklin swam for an hour in the pool. He could feel his toes moving and happily told his friends that he walked around in water four feet deep without braces or crutches, almost as well as if his legs were healing. A reporter from *The Atlanta Journal*, Cleburne Gregory, spent a few days with Franklin and Missy there in 1924. The journal's photos showed Franklin in his bathing suit, sitting on a towel, his legs atrophied but his upper body strong and agile. His face was always smiling. "Franklin D. Roosevelt," wrote the journalist, "is literally swimming back to health and strength in Warm Springs."

Eleanor, who believed that Franklin would never walk again, tried to convince him that buying Warm Springs was a waste of money. The owner of the springs, George Foster Peabody, asked for $195,000, a sum that seemed outrageous to her. Nonetheless, Franklin insisted that the springs, and the people who came to the springs from all over the country after Gregory's article was published, might become a medical opportunity for the many people who suffered from polio. In time, he paid the asking price and bought Warm Springs from Peabody.

Franklin and Eleanor had given each other the space to cultivate romantic friendships and to have sexual relationships outside of the marriage. FDR had Missy LeHand, who functioned as a second wife. Eleanor realized she also needed intimate friends she could depend upon: Esther Lape and Elizabeth Read in the Village, Nancy Cook and Marion Dickerman at Val-Kill.

But the Val-Kill relationship became complicated. Nancy and Marion were taken in by FDR, which interfered with their loyalty to Eleanor. Nancy and Marion both wanted to be near this charming man, and instead they got in between Franklin and Eleanor. Eleanor grew unhappy with the two women. She and Franklin had different ideas and opinions at times. Eleanor was concerned that the two women were revealing her differing opinions to Franklin and felt they were no longer trustworthy. On frequent occasions when Nancy, Marion, Franklin, and Eleanor were all at Hyde Park, Eleanor stayed in the Big House and not in her room in the Val-Kill cottage with Nancy and Marion.

In 1926 Nancy and Marion decided to open a furniture factory on the grounds of Val-Kill. Eleanor and Caroline O'Day, a wealthy suffragist and friend from the Democratic State Committee, supported and helped fund the project. Nancy took charge of the idea and went to several places for inspiration—the Metropolitan Museum of Art in New York, the Chicago and Hartford Museums, and later to Monticello, Thomas Jefferson's plantation near Charlottesville, Virginia. She pored over the project, hovering over her bottles and jars of stain in search of just the right one, and every piece of furniture was polished until the wood had the texture and velvety glow she wanted. Eleanor drew from her own earnings and paid for Nancy's work.

Their first furniture projects were designed for Franklin's new cottage in Warm Springs and intrigued him. "The furniture from the Val-Kill show is a great success," he wrote to Eleanor. By the spring of 1927, Franklin and Eleanor were exhibiting furniture pieces from Val-Kill at the Roosevelt house on 65th Street in New York. The prices ranged from $40 for trestle tables to $175 for a large maple chest of drawers. "The work is hand-wrought and beautifully finished in every detail and copied with exactness from genuine antiques," wrote *The New York Times*.

The high-quality reproduction of Early American furniture produced at Val-Kill was a success, but Eleanor was not as interested in the work as Nancy was. Instead, she looked for other outlets that would satisfy her needs.

Marion was a teacher and vice principal of the Todhunter School, a private finishing school for girls on East 89th Street in New York City. Winifred Todhunter, a graduate of Oxford University, had founded the school but moved back to England in 1927. The school also provided preparation for college, and most of its students were wealthy young women from New York. Marion did not have the money to buy the school, but Eleanor, who had always wanted to teach, loaned Marion what she needed. Marion served as principal and asked Eleanor to take the title of associate principal, but Eleanor declined because she lacked a college degree.

The start of the school day was traditional. At ten minutes of nine, the hundred uniformed girls, from ages five to eighteen, walked to the assembly room "to a stirring march on the piano," a writer from New York who witnessed the process reported. Eleanor and Marion, "stately figures in tailored dark red gowns and low-heeled oxfords, . . . stand behind a long table in front to receive them. There is a hymn, a prayer and announcements. . . . Then comes another song of the girls' own choosing, which may be as popular as they please. The morning I was there they sang 'Polly-wolly-doodle' with great relish."

Like her mentor, Souvestre, Eleanor encouraged students to think for themselves and to do their homework. In the first year, a few of her senior girls came to school unprepared. She wrote to Franklin in February 1928, after her first semester at Todhunter, "I can't say I am set up by the example my children did. I only flunked one but the others were none too good." She wanted her students to do better and demonstrated the lessons she had learned from Souvestre, who had taught her to believe that the main thing in education "is the interest around a young mind by a stimulating, vivid personality." Eleanor's message to her students was: "Be Somebody. Be Yourself. Be All You Can

Be." She had found her own life among the well-educated women in Greenwich Village and wanted to share that life.

Eleanor loved the Todhunter School and gave the young women all that she had learned. She taught courses in American history, American literature, drama, and English. She had kept her Allenswood notebooks and found them useful. She taught students to study the classics. "Who was your favorite character in *Midsummer Night's Dream* and your favorite characters in *Twelfth Night*?" she asked. Her drama course began with Aeschylus and ended with Eugene O'Neill. Her own favorite authors were Charles Dickens, Robert Browning, and Walt Whitman. Students were also taught to answer questions such as: "Give your reasons for or against allowing women to actively participate in the control of the government, politics and officials through the vote, as well as your reasons for or against women holding office in the government."

Eleanor's questions for her students reflected her political concerns: "Do you know of any way in which the Government protects women and children?" "What is the difference between civil and political liberty?" "What is the World Court?" "How are Negroes excluded from voting in the South?"

She took students on field trips to visit courthouses and also to tenements in the city, so they could see the problems faced by poor New Yorkers. In addition, she took them to the Neighborhood Playhouse, founded in 1915, and introduced the senior girls to the Women's Trade Union League.

If the young women from Todhunter had been given access in their day to the Myers-Briggs test, a personality test developed by Isabel Briggs Myers and Katharine Cook Briggs in the 1940s, they would not have been surprised if Eleanor's type turned out to be INFP—introverted, intuitive, feeling, and perceptive. In time, she overcame her introverted personality when she was in the classroom with her teenage students. The liberal ideas she espoused did not come from her own personal upbringing or from her experience as a full-time mother and wife. They came from her transformation among friends and associates in Greenwich Village.

In New York, Eleanor divided her time between the Todhunter School uptown and the political and social mix of Greenwich Village. By 1927, many lesbians resided in the Village. When Nancy and Marion were in town, they lived across the hall from Molly Dewson, a powerful leader of the Democratic Party, and Dewson's partner, Mary Polly Porter, who described herself as a "poetic anarchist." Polly was close to two leading Communist Party members, Grace Hutchins and Anna Rochester, who shared an apartment in the same building, at 171 West 12th Street. Molly Dewson served as president of the New York Consumers' League, and played a central role in the passage of a 1930 New York law limiting women to forty-eight-hour workweeks.

In addition to her close women friends, Eleanor tended to associate with writers such as Thomas Wolfe, who shared a room on the top floor of a dilapidated building at 13 East 8th Street with his mistress, Aline Bernstein, where he wrote *Look Homeward, Angel*. Eleanor knew Fannie Hurst, a feminist and novelist who wrote a classic early novel about race, *Imitation of Life*. Jackson Pollock, the celebrated painter of abstract expressionist art, was introduced to Eleanor by her wealthy friend Gertrude Vanderbilt Whitney, who in 1931 founded the Whitney Museum of American Art.

In 1929, Franklin became governor of New York, and Eleanor was stretched in many directions. She continued her three-day teaching schedule at the Todhunter School, and then took the train from Grand Central Terminal to Albany, preparing her next week's classes on the train. "I teach because I love it, I cannot give it up," she once told a reporter, "because it is the one thing that belongs to me."

CHAPTER 13

The Governor's Mansion

Great minds discuss ideas. Average minds discuss events.
Small minds discuss people.
—*Eleanor Roosevelt*

B y the time Franklin D. Roosevelt was elected governor of New York State in 1928, Eleanor had made
an independent life for herself, a life she was determined
to continue. She realized she would have to carry on in
public as the governor's wife but refused to give up her
teaching schedule. She realized that her life in Albany
would be difficult, but she and Franklin had made a deal;
while she would be the governor's wife, she would also
pursue her own agenda—a life that served her needs as
an activist.

On the tenth of November 1928, *The New York Times*
ran an article headlined, "Mrs. Roosevelt to Keep on Fill-
ing Many Jobs Besides Being the 'First Lady' at Albany."
Eleanor stated that her teaching was important to her,
but she did not tell the press that she was considering giv-

ing up politics. Questions were asked about how Eleanor would arrange her life to be available to her children. She explained that John, her youngest son, had joined Franklin Jr. and Elliott at Groton, and James was at Harvard. She assured the press in a motherly tone of voice that she would keep her eyes on her boys even though they were no longer living at home.

Her role as first lady at Albany was restricted to making the executive mansion into a home for her husband, her children when home from school, and guests. The statehouse was large and adorned with turrets and cupolas, its interior hallway walls covered in red paper. The first thing that Eleanor did was to provide more suitable quarters for the servants, who had previously had a small and cramped space for eating. There was also the issue of what to do with the many animals that FDR's predecessor, Governor Alfred E. Smith, had left behind—three monkeys, one elk, one deer, one fawn, and six dogs. Eleanor removed three greenhouses, which grew beautiful flowers but cost $6,000 a year. Cautious about spending money, Eleanor replaced the greenhouses with a heated pool for Franklin's daily exercises.

For FDR's bedroom, Eleanor chose the "grandest sunny room" in the mansion, a corner room on the second floor. The library was downstairs and served as a family workroom. Eleanor gave Missy a room with a single bed. It made sense; after all, Missy spent more time with FDR than Eleanor did. When Franklin had official guests in the mansion and Eleanor was not there, FDR told Missy to act as mistress of the mansion. Eleanor had a small sitting room for herself, but it did not have a bed. On the days when she was in Albany, she would use the sitting room during the day and sleep in a servant's room on the third floor at night.

Week after week, Eleanor was teacher, mother, and part-time mistress of the mansion, and went back and forth from Albany to New York City. She was not a romantic schoolgirl anymore, but an engaged political wife. Previously, in May 1927, she had published an article in *Success Magazine* that remains useful in today's world. She encouraged women to follow politics to "guard against the emptiness and loneliness that enter some women's lives after their children are grown." She wrote that women needed to have "lives, interests and personalities of their own apart from their households." Eleanor was speaking from her heart about her mother-in-law and the lonely days she, Eleanor, experienced on her own.

In the months after Franklin contracted polio, Eleanor had championed his return to political life, and by 1928 had even substituted for him at New York Democratic Party rallies while he was in the waters of Florida or discovering the healing potential of Warm Springs. Because they had agreed that Eleanor was free to move into public life and work on the causes that were important to her, when FDR was campaigning for governor of New York, she knew more people than Franklin, an indication that she was needed to help him continue to thrive in politics.

However, her focus in campaigning was on helping Al Smith win the presidency. Smith's defeat hurt Eleanor at every level, as it was a rejection of the social programs she had championed. She had the foresight to see that progressives would have to step back, reorganize, and rethink their strategy before the 1932 elections.

On the other hand, Sara vigorously supported her son in the gubernatorial election. She previously had wanted to take care of him forever at Hyde Park, but Franklin finally convinced her that politics was his only way back to health. A month before the election she wrote a note to FDR saying: "I do not want you to be defeated." Privately she assured him "all will be well" if he should win.

The race was close, and the results were not known until 4 a.m. the day after the election. Franklin won by just more than 25,000 votes, while Al Smith lost the state of New York by 103,481 votes. A Republican landslide throughout the country insured that Herbert Hoover easily won the presidency.

On January 1, 1929, in Albany, with the streets covered in snow, FDR was inaugurated governor of New York for a two-year term. With a seventeenth-century Dutch Bible in his hand, Franklin took his oath of office in the same room in which Theodore Roosevelt had been sworn in as governor of New York thirty years before, at the age of forty. Franklin was forty-six.

According to Hazel Rowley in her biography *Franklin and Eleanor: An Extraordinary Marriage*, Sara Delano

Roosevelt proudly attended the ceremony and told her friends that her son had finally "grown up." But Rowley's analysis suggests that the generosity of Franklin's mother also diminished FDR's authority in the eyes of his family. With an annual salary of $10,000 (approximately $150,000 today), his income as governor was not enough to support a large family as well as to position FDR for his next step: the presidency. Writes Rowley:

> Sara had been forty-six when she inherited her husband's estate and took control of Hyde Park—the same age as FDR when he became governor. For the rest of her life—she lived to the age of eighty-six—Sara would give money to Franklin and his family. She had the satisfaction of knowing that her generosity made her son's political career possible. But she was never willing to do the one thing that would give Franklin his independence. She never increased the trust fund Franklin's father had left him, and she never turned over to him any of her capital. . . . As Eleanor saw it, Franklin had generously made his mother part of his life. In response, Mama took away much of his authority as a husband and father, humiliating Franklin in front of his family. Eleanor could never forgive her for this abuse of power.

Eleanor and Louis Howe often met at Sara's home on East 65th Street to talk politics, discuss future political appointments, and plan strategy. Eleanor and FDR depended on Howe to facilitate discussion of their political differences. For example, Eleanor was very attuned to poverty, especially in the South and Appalachia. She also felt strongly about racial inequalities. For Franklin it would have been politically difficult to speak up for racial equality for fear of losing support in southern states—and the votes of southern Democrats in Congress. While Franklin was in Warm Springs, Howe was not surprised that Al Smith hoped Roosevelt's physical disability and perhaps insecurity would allow Smith to recommend one of his own close associates as FDR's secretary. Smith tried to push Belle Moskowitz, his closest adviser and publicist, into a top position on FDR's political team.

Eleanor was not shy in protecting Franklin. With Louis Howe by her side, she told FDR, "You have to decide and you have to decide it now, whether you are going to be Governor of this state, or whether Mrs. Moskowitz is going to be Governor of this state. If Mrs. Moskowitz is your secretary, she will ruin you." She understood that Franklin did not like to be the messenger of bad news. "Don't let Mrs. M. get draped around you for she means to be," she wrote in a letter to him in Warm Springs. "It will always be one for you and two for Al." FDR stood up to Al Smith and did not include Moskowitz on his team.

Even before Franklin assumed the office, Eleanor suggested that he consider making Frances Perkins the labor commissioner for New York State. "She will do well and you could fill her place as chair of the Industrial Commission by one of the men . . . and put Nell Schwartz (Bureau of Women in Industry) on the commission so there will be one woman on it. These are suggestions which I am passing on not my opinions, for I don't want to butt in." Perkins was a progressive reformer who had earlier worked vigorously to end child labor and to provide safety for women workers. It was a brave move for FDR to put a woman in charge of the Department of Labor. Franklin trusted Eleanor and boasted to Perkins, "I've got more nerve about women and their status in the world than Al has." Again Eleanor had his back.

FDR decided that Eleanor needed to use the governor's limousine for her many official trips, but Eleanor refused. She was determined to drive her own car. In 1929, FDR assigned Earl Miller to act as her bodyguard. Miller, a handsome thirty-one-year-old former amateur welterweight champion, an instructor in judo and boxing, and a circus acrobat, was a self-described Romeo. He was an orphan from a modest family background who left home at the age of twelve. As it happened, Eleanor had been orphaned at ten years old and never forgot her lonely years as a child. The two established a bond.

Miller called Eleanor "Lady" and Franklin "the Boss." Eleanor liked his company. He did not tease her about her lack of driving skills, but his driving lessons allowed her to overcome her fear behind the wheel. They played tennis and rode horses together. Miller gave Eleanor a horse she named Dot, a compliant chestnut mare. She loved the horse and was soon riding. One day in Warm Springs, Earl put FDR in the saddle on Dot and held "the Boss" tightly so he would not fall. Franklin called out to the press to come quick to take photos and gave them his best smile. It was yet another way to show them that, in his mind at least, Franklin was beating polio.

For the next four years Eleanor traveled all over the state with Earl Miller, who became fiercely loyal to her. Sometimes FDR came along, but he stayed in the car, touring the grounds and talking to the press. Meanwhile Eleanor, whom FDR described as his "eyes and legs," went to hospitals, asylums, and state prisons. Eleanor was determined to note the thoughts of the patients about the staff. In two years, FDR and Eleanor toured and inspected multiple sites in the state with Miller's help. Eleanor despised having her photograph taken. At her height, she had to bend down to face the camera, and Earl was the only one who could make her smile in front of reporters. He convinced her she had a beautiful smile and face and joked with her as he stood behind the photographers, making faces that made her laugh. Later, when Earl was not around, she continued to work on her smile for the cameras.

Eleanor's mother-in-law did not approve of Earl; she found him too rough and he did not know how to speak clearly and with gusto. Marion Dickerman and Nancy Cook also had no use for Earl. "He used to annoy me the way he talked to her," said Marion. "I didn't like his tone of voice, sometimes, when he told Eleanor what to do or when he did not like what was being served at the table." Earl went everywhere with Eleanor. He had a room at Val-Kill, and also in the apartment that Eleanor rented on East 11th Street in the Village.

As with Franklin's relationship with Missy, in which she was sixteen years younger than he, Earl was thirteen years younger than Eleanor. He shared Eleanor's commitment to progressive politics but there was more to it than that. Eleanor was in love with Earl for some time but kept the affair a secret from her children. For instance, her son James was twenty-two when he first saw his mother with Earl. He didn't seem to mind the relationship:

"Mother was self-conscious about Miller's youth, but he did not seem bothered by the difference in age. He encouraged her to take pride in herself, to be unafraid of facing the world. He did a lot of good for her. She seemed to draw strength from him when he was by her side, and she came to rely on him. When she had problems, she sought his help. . . . He became part of the family, too, and gave her a great deal of what her husband and we, her sons, failed to give her. Above all, he made her feel that she was a woman."

If his father noticed, he did not seem to mind. Curiously, he did promote a romance between Miller and Missy, but that did not last. Miller, who'd previously had an unhappy first marriage, later married a cousin of his first wife. That ended the gossip about Eleanor and him. But this was not a happy marriage either.

"All the while," James wrote, "Miller had continued

131

to see Mother and frequently was a guest at Val-Kill. He saw other women, too, and she encouraged his romances. He married a third time in 1941, though he continued to see Mother regularly. This marriage was a failure, too. . . . Maybe because of Mother. Their relationship deepened after Father's death and ended only with Mother's death."

Eleanor and Earl wrote hundreds of letters to each other over the long years they were together. Like many other important things in Eleanor's life, the letters were destroyed, probably by Eleanor herself. There are some photographs and home movies, but no memoirs, no letters to explain one of the most important parts of Eleanor's life. Joseph Lash, Eleanor's personal biographer, described her relationship with Earl in mother-and-son terms. Lash himself was another son for Eleanor and naturally did not see her in the same way that Eleanor saw Earl, as a woman in love, who enjoyed being called "Dearest Lady."

While Lash and others might not have considered Eleanor a sexually interesting woman because of her age, Earl was one of the few men in her life who found her physically desirable. She enjoyed herself with Earl; he flirted with her and made her laugh, he took her for walks atop the Adirondack Mountains and other places. He gave her a private life—the freedom to go out on her own. If that wasn't love, it would have to do.

The relationship between Eleanor and Earl Miller transpired because the Roosevelts had an open marriage, kept secret by their advisers and close friends. It is difficult to imagine that modern-day Americans would somehow remain blind to the fact that a president had affairs with women while his first lady had significant relationships with both women and men. Yet Franklin and Eleanor did just that, and the public remained unaware. The press at the time was forgiving to both of them. But what kept the Roosevelts together? Their family, their duty to their country, and their desire to be at the cutting edge of politics.

Eleanor had once believed that she and Franklin would have a bright future until she found Lucy Mercer's love letters to her husband. Eleanor wondered if she should stay in the marriage and focus on helping other women's lives or whether should she leave Franklin, who by then was determined to become president. Eleanor decided to stay with her husband. Much later, first lady Lady Bird Johnson was confronted with a similar issue and remained in the marriage. Hillary Rodham Clinton was another first lady who faced such a crisis and followed Eleanor's lead, staying in her difficult marriage.

CHAPTER 14

Eleanor Roosevelt's Erotic Relationship

Do what you feel in your heart to be right,
for you will be criticized anyway.
—*Eleanor Roosevelt*

E arl Miller was not the only person who understood that Eleanor was inherently shy and needed affection. In 1932, as Franklin ran for president, Eleanor began a lesbian relationship with Lorena Alice Hickok, a respected newspaperwoman known as "Hick," who worked for the Washington Bureau of the Associated Press. They met on October 30, 1932, aboard the *Roosevelt Special*, a six-car campaign train Franklin used. It was a cold and rainy evening, and Eleanor invited Hick into her private car, which had a lower berth and a narrow couch. The two talked as the train rolled along and in time stopped in the small town of Potsdam, New York, not too far from the Canadian border. The mother of Missy LeHand had died in Potsdam, and Eleanor got off the train to pay her respects and attend the burial. As Blanche Wiesen Cook explains, Eleanor treated Missy with affection, despite her jealousy. She thought of Missy as her daughter, which made for a complex relationship. To some degree, Missy's presence at the White House made it possible for Eleanor to pursue her own interests. Missy wrote all the president's private letters, paid the bills, and balanced his checkbook.

Hick later wrote in an unfinished manuscript that it was on that trip to Potsdam that Eleanor and Hickok's relationship became intimate:

> I did not go to the funeral, but spent the time walking around the town. . . . Later Mrs. Roosevelt looked me up at the restaurant where I was having lunch. She had borrowed an automobile and asked if I'd like to go for a drive. . . .
>
> We dined with some of her friends that night. And when we boarded our train, the only space available was one drawing room. . . . To my embarrassment, Mrs. Roosevelt insisted on giving me the lower berth, and took for herself the long, narrow couch on the other side of the drawing room.
>
> "I'm longer than you are," Eleanor said when I protested. "And," she added with a grin, "not quite so broad!"
>
> It was early, neither of us were sleepy, and so we started talking.

That night they slept very little and stayed up sharing childhood stories. Hick told Eleanor about her abusive father. Eleanor told Hick about her alcoholic father, her disapproving mother, her overbearing grandmother, and that her aunts had called her "the ugly duckling." Eleanor also told Hick about Marie Souvestre and her time at the Allenswood school.

As Hickok remembered it, Eleanor did most of the talking.

> "May I write some of that?" I asked her fearfully before we said good night.
> "If you like," responded Eleanor, "I trust you."

Hick had many friends in New York and plenty of money. She earned cash playing poker with hard-boiled newspapermen, whom she loved to laugh with, while she constantly smoked cigarettes and sometimes enjoyed cigars. Eleanor, soon to be the reluctant first lady, and Hickok talked endlessly about their differences and their plans for the future. In time, they recognized that the two of them had important things in common. Both had lost their mothers at an early age, both saw themselves as unattractive and unloved. And both were determined to achieve great success in their chosen careers—politics for Eleanor and journalism for Hick. Hickok told Eleanor a childhood secret that she had suppressed for many years: her father had not only abused and beaten her, his adolescent daughter, but had also raped her. When Eleanor realized Hickok's situation, she was shocked and embraced Hick to comfort her.

On Election Day, FDR carried forty-two of the forty-eight states, thereby ending twelve years of Republican rule and setting into motion what would become one of the most critically important presidencies in the history of the republic.

Reporters surrounded Eleanor and asked if she was pleased to become first lady. "Of course, I'm pleased," Eleanor said. "You're always pleased to have someone you're devoted to have what he wants." Despite Eleanor's newfound love for Hick, her loyalty to FDR did not waver. Their long-standing bargain to move forward together in political life remained intact.

In time, Hick gave up her job and moved into the White House to work for Eleanor. It was Hick who told Eleanor that she should invite women journalists to the White House, and on March 6, 1933, the Monday after the inauguration, thirty-five female reporters came to the Red Room. "There weren't enough chairs to go around, so some had to sit on the floor," Eleanor told Hick. For many years from then on, weekly White House press conferences for women journalists were held.

Who was this bulky, rough-edged woman who fell in love with Eleanor, this wealthy, crusading leftist surrounded by independent women, many of whom were lesbians? Hick had been born into poverty in East Troy,

Wisconsin, in 1893. She spent her childhood traveling the upper Midwest, where her father, a butter maker, looked for work from town to town. In 1907, when Hickok was fourteen years old, her mother died, which forced Hick to leave home to earn her own living. She traveled from place to place and was always the new girl in town looking for work. She was lonely, hungry for both food and affection. As she wrote in an unfinished book, during a two-year period she worked with nine different employers. Four of the nine fired her. Nonetheless, Hickok was grateful to be away from her abusive father.

When Hickok turned sixteen, her mother's cousin Ella Ellis wrote and asked her to come and live with her in her own home. Hick didn't hesitate. Ellis sent her railroad fare for Michigan, and from that moment on Hickok's employment prospects improved. She enrolled in high school in Battle Creek, Michigan, and although not pretty, she was the tallest and smartest in her class. In time, she became a reporter for the *Battle Creek Evening News*, an important accomplishment for a young woman of her time. Later, in Minneapolis, she lived for eight years with her lover Ella Morse, who worked on the society section of the newspaper.

From 1928 to 1933, Hick worked in the New York Bureau of the Associated Press and covered New York state politics. In time, Eleanor invited her to tea at the 65th Street home when Hick was first assigned to interview Eleanor. "I watched with fascination the graceful way she manipulated the tea things with her long slender hands. She was wearing a lace-trimmed hostess gown considerably more becoming than things I had seen her wearing around headquarters." They ended up discussing their dogs in detail and spoke little of politics during that initial encounter.

In those days, lesbian relationships were not commonly recognized by the outside world and were carried out in secret. For example, one of the first lesbian autobiographies was published in 1930 under the pseudonym of Mary Casal. The writer and her female lover later wrote that the two of them believed they were the only women in the world who loved another woman. Nine years later, Frances V. Rummell published *Diana: A Strange Autobiography*, in which two lesbians live happily together. Rummell was a well-known French teacher. In 1939, Eleanor met her in New York City and wrote about their meeting for her "My Day" column, which appeared six days a week and was syndicated all over the country. It was Hick who had brought Rummell and Eleanor together.

By the time of FDR's elevation to the presidency, Eleanor had long found strength among lesbians, many of them in Greenwich Village, women who were wealthy and not dependent on husbands. These friends included the aforementioned Esther Lape, Elizabeth Read, Nancy Cook, and Marion Dickerson, but also included Molly Dewson and Mary Dreier, who each had female partners. It might have astonished some that even the eventual secretary of labor, Frances Perkins, married to an invalid husband, had a female companion. Perhaps it was inevitable that Eleanor, whom Hick called "First Friend," would become a couple as well.

When Eleanor and Hick were both in New York, they spent time together attending plays, concerts, and operas. In Manhattan, Hick lived in a thirteen-story apartment building at 10 Mitchell Place, two blocks from what would later become the UN headquarters near the East River, and only a block away from what would later become FDR Drive, the wide highway that courses up the island's east side. She frequently made dinner for Eleanor. At other times, she accompanied Eleanor to Sara Roosevelt's 65th Street house, Franklin and Eleanor's home when they first married. How the times had changed; Eleanor and FDR were now engaged in a political marriage rather than a love match.

When the two women were not together, Eleanor dialed WI2-6131, Hick's telephone number in New York, to chat. Hickok had always lived a public life, but she clearly understood the importance of protecting Eleanor in their relationship. Nonetheless, as the first lady of the United States, Eleanor took enormous risks that could have exposed either one of them. In some of her letters, it is clear that Eleanor felt passionately for Hick.

Coinciding with Franklin's first inauguration as president on March 4, 1933, Eleanor became the nation's thirty-fourth first lady and was determined to find a new role for that position at the White House, one that would be meaningful to her. At the end of the following day, on Hick's fortieth birthday, Eleanor sent off a letter to her from the White House that said:

"Hick darling, All day I've thought of you & another birthday I *will* be with you & yet tonite you sounded so far away & formal. Oh! I want to put my arms around you, I ache to hold you close. Your ring is a great comfort. I look at it and think she does love me, or I wouldn't be wearing it . . . All my love."

The ring was sapphire, given to Eleanor by Hickok.

On March 6, Eleanor wrote again: "Hick darling, Oh! How good it was to hear your voice; it was so inadequate to try and tell you what it meant, Jimmy [her son James] was near & I couldn't say . . . *je t'aime et je 'adore'* as I longed to but always remember I am saying it & that I go to sleep thinking of you & repeat our little saying."

In the early years of their relationship, Hick felt she needed Eleanor, and became determined to give her confidence. Hick was not ashamed that she was a lesbian. However, some writers have concluded that because of Eleanor's early life she was unable to express her emotional needs in a sexual manner to anyone. Often, Eleanor fell into a mood of deep depression. There is no doubt that Hick loved Eleanor, but if Eleanor was unable to express her sexual feelings to herself, how could she relate them to Hick? It became difficult for each of them to balance what they needed.

"Darling," wrote Eleanor, "I've been thinking about you so much today. What a swell person you are to back me up the way you do on this job! We do things together, don't we? And it's fun, even though the fact that we both have work to do keeps us apart."

And later Hick wrote this to Eleanor: "I've been trying today to bring back your face. Most clearly I remember your eyes, with a kind of teasing smile in them and the feeling of that soft spot just northeast of the corner of your mouth against my lips."

CHAPTER 15

Eleanor as First Lady

Campaign behavior for wives: Always be on time.
Do as little talking as humanly possible. Lean back
in the parade car so everybody can see the president.
—*Eleanor Roosevelt*

O n February 15, 1933, a few weeks before Roosevelt
was inaugurated as president, he took a trip to Miami
in order to cruise on Vincent Astor's yacht. FDR was in
a good mood; since boyhood nothing made him happier
than to be at sea. After the boat had docked, FDR's staff
helped him into the backseat of a convertible so that he
could meet the crowd that had come to see him. He flashed
his usual wide grin and made a speech. People gathered
around the car to shake his hand. In the next moment,
an Italian immigrant, Giuseppe Zangara, stepped up on a
chair and opened fire with a .35-caliber pistol. Several by-
standers were hit, including the mayor of Chicago, Anton
Cermak, who was wounded in the chest. The Secret Service swarmed the president-elect, who told them to rush
Cermak to the hospital. FDR held Cermak and talked to

him until they got there. "I'm glad it was me instead of you," Cermak told him. Three weeks later Cermak died.

The world was a dangerous place, but it was time to inaugurate a new president. Saturday, March 4, 1933, was cold and windy, a blustery, blue day in every possible way. The press covered each detail of Eleanor Roosevelt's wardrobe: her blue velvet dress, her hat (also blue), her white kid gloves, the smart eight-button length. At forty-eight years of age, Eleanor stood at five feet, eleven inches, only two inches shorter than her husband. She was trim and willowy, her thick blond hair tucked beneath her cap, her gentle blue eyes wide open to the world. She would not know it that day, but Eleanor would go on to serve as first lady through four terms of an FDR presidency, making her the longest serving first lady in history.

At 10 a.m. Eleanor and Franklin and their eldest son, James, went to St. John's Episcopal Church, across Lafayette Square from the White House. They were greeted by Reverend Endicott Peabody, rector of the private Groton School, who had officiated at Eleanor and Franklin's wedding twenty-eight years before in New York. The irony was not lost on Eleanor, who had not shared her husband's bed for the past fifteen years.

On Inauguration Day, Eleanor worried that Roosevelt's election as president would mark the end of her own hard-won independence. As much as she shared FDR's ideas and plans for the country's future, she feared she would become beholden to the routine, obligatory duties of the first lady.

Before the election, Eleanor confided in her women friends in Greenwich Village that she could not bring herself to live full-time in the White House. Wrote Eleanor: "As I saw it, this meant the end of any meaningful personal life of my own." As things worked out, she made regular visits to her apartment in the same building where Esther Lape and Elizabeth Read lived, and somehow managed to keep her secrets from newspapers and photographers the entire time she served as first lady.

Just before noon on March 4, Eleanor and Franklin appeared together on the East Portico of the Capitol. With his son's help, Franklin inched his polio-ravaged legs down the red-carpeted ramp. The crowd watched in silence out of respect and hope for the newly elected president.

Eleanor stood beside Franklin as he was sworn in. "Her pale face and austere demeanor bore testimony to the solemnity with which she viewed Mr. Roosevelt's new position," Emma Bugbee reported in the *New York Herald Tribune* the following morning. "Many friends watched for an opportunity to wave to her, and strangers trained cameras upon her, but not once did she lift her eyes to the crowd or wave her hand or smile." In Eleanor's mind this was a solemn day.

In 1933 the country was in the depths of the Great Depression. The unemployment rate in the United States on Inauguration Day stood at 25 percent of the nation's workforce, or about fifteen million jobless. Among farms in Mississippi, 40 percent were on the auction block. American farmers had not shared in the prosperity of the "Roaring Twenties": even before the stock market crash of October 1929, during the 1920s farm bankruptcies had multiplied fivefold, and hundreds of rural banks had failed. Since the crash the financial distress had only deepened. By the time Roosevelt took office, 50 percent of the people in Harlem were out of work. Settlement houses in Greenwich Village doled out thin soup to the unemployed. Eleanor had held two benefit fund-raisers for working artists at Romany Marie's tavern in Greenwich Village. Marie and Eleanor ladled out free soup for her friends through the Depression, so that the tavern was also a soup kitchen. Eleanor worked hands-on preparing and serving the soup.

She had crisscrossed the country, often with Hick, and had seen the effects of the Depression: schools closed, coal miners out of work, hobos on trains, children hungry. She was aware of the national crisis and was determined to be a driving force to change the country. Much to her husband's occasional distress, Eleanor was a strong-willed woman. But now sometimes it was as if all that she had done in the last two decades to free herself and develop her own identity were about to be torn away from her. "My zest in life is rather gone for the time being," Eleanor wrote to Hick. "If anyone looks at me, I want to weep."

On Sunday, March 12, FDR gave his first "fireside chat" via national radio at 10 p.m. All over the country, men and women sat down around their radios and waited for the speech. Although Calvin Coolidge in December 1923 had been the first president to address the nation by radio (then a recent invention), until Roosevelt's talks there had not been a sustained program of broadcasting from the White House. In this first address, on the national banking system and the financial remedies his administration was implementing, FDR concentrated on the people he imagined would be listening to him, the common man and woman worried about the jobs and money lost in the Great Depression. When he spoke, FDR promised his listeners that he would put an end to the Depression by reopening the nation's banks. Six days before, on March 6, Congress had passed the Emergency Banking Act, creating the Federal Deposit Insurance Corporation (FDIC) for insuring bank deposits. He asked all who could hear him to take their money back to the banks. "I can assure you, my friends, that it is safer to keep your money in a reopened bank than it is to keep it under the mattress. . . . We have provided the machinery to restore our financial system; it is up to you to support it and make it work. It is your problem no less than it is mine. Together we cannot fail."

During his first seven years in the White House Roosevelt delivered thirteen fireside chats that were extremely effective in communicating with American citizens. Some of his advisers thought he should deliver these chats monthly; FDR realized that presenting them too frequently would in fact make less of an impact. He focused on the banking crisis, the currency, and the New Deal and Works Relief programs, and in later talks he covered such topics as the unemployment census, the drought in the Great Plains, and the war in Europe.

Eleanor assisted FDR with White House correspondence, but what she wanted was to work outside of the White House in order to do something more worthwhile. In mid-August 1933, Harry Hopkins, a close friend who had served as chairman of the New York State Temporary Emergency Relief Administration established by then Governor Roosevelt, was in charge of the Federal Emergency Relief Administration (FERA), and, upon Eleanor's recommendation, asked Hick to organize help for those living in rural America. Hick resigned from her job with the Associated Press in 1933 and sought out Clarence Pickett, an executive secretary of the American Friends Service Committee, the political action organization of the Quakers, to assist her.

It was Pickett who told Hick, "Go down to the southwest part of the state [Pennsylvania] and into West Virginia." Hick traveled to Appalachia and realized that Pickett had not exaggerated the depths of poverty and distress. Hick was alarmed to see the faces of many fathers black with coal. Children and their parents were forced to drink grimy water. Everyone was hungry. The poverty was difficult to fathom. Hick quickly wrote to Eleanor, told her what she saw, and Eleanor decided to go and see Appalachia for herself. It was a big step toward the New Deal.

Eleanor drove alone in her shiny blue car from Washington to Morgantown, West Virginia. She had refused to allow the Secret Service to come along. When she arrived in West Virginia, she saw hundreds of miners and their families who had been stranded in the state when the mines were permanently closed. She met up with Hick in Morgantown. The two of them went from place to place, listening to people talk about their circumstances. Eleanor and Hick stopped at one house and talked to an out-of-work miner who showed Eleanor his last paycheck was less than a dollar a week. There were six children in his house, all of them hungry.

Eleanor and FDR talked about how to resettle men like that miner and get them back to work. Franklin told Eleanor that he would help, but it was her responsibility to create a New Deal for the miners. A new town was built on a farm in West Virginia, called Arthurdale. Once the structures were completed, fifty families were settled in new homes, on the promise that they would repay the government over fifty years. With Eleanor's backing, successfully raising funds for the project from her wealthy friends, the government built a clinic, a school, a carpentry shop, a community center, and fifty farmhouses. For three years the town of Arthurdale was Eleanor's personal project. The launch of the town was such a success that other communities followed its lead. Often Eleanor sat with the homesteaders on their porches and talked to them about what they needed.

Eleanor spent Thanksgiving of 1933 with FDR and his friends at Warm Springs. On Christmas Day she stayed with Franklin and her children at the White House. Hick reluctantly decided to leave the Roosevelts to their own devices and took the train to New York. "I went to sleep saying a little prayer," Eleanor wrote Hick on December 23. "God give me depth enough to never hurt Hick again." But of course she did hurt her again. The relationship was changing such that Hick, no longer employed by the AP, relied almost entirely on Eleanor for work prospects. Due to her well-known friendship with Eleanor, Hick's career as a journalist had to be set aside. Eleanor subsequently arranged a position for Hick in the Federal Emergency Relief Administration in 1933, where she would serve as chief investigator until 1936.

Eleanor's commitment to women's full recognition and participation in politics and business was intense. She worked with women's groups around the nation to build their political base. In 1936, Eleanor and Molly Dewson organized a lobbying effort created by 219 women delegates and 302 women alternates. "Women must learn to play the games as men do," said Eleanor. "Otherwise we won't win."

Eleanor also spent time in the Village. She enjoyed being in the middle of it all, and fought against segregation, as a result making many black friends in Greenwich Village. For instance, the American Communist Party played an important role in the labor movement against lynching. Eleanor took a trip to the South, where she saw that African Americans were discriminated against at every turn. Eleanor pushed hard for legislation to ensure the end to lynching laws—and made some progress.

Eleanor first met Marian Anderson, a famous African American opera singer, in 1935 when Anderson performed at the White House. The contralto was already well known in Europe, where her skin color was less of an impediment to a professional singing career. When Howard University asked the Daughters of the American Revolution's permission for Anderson to sing at Constitution Hall for her popular annual concert to benefit the university's school of music, the DAR, all wealthy white women, refused. Eleanor was furious and quickly resigned her membership in the DAR, a bold thing for a first lady to do. In her "My Day" column the following day, February 27, Eleanor wrote, without naming the organization, "To remain as a member implies approval of that action, therefore I am resigning."

Instead, Eleanor arranged for Anderson to sing on the steps of the Lincoln Memorial. Where an audience of four thousand might have filled Constitution Hall, a crowd of some seventy-five thousand gathered at the Lincoln Memorial on a cold day in early April 1939. Two months later, Marian Anderson sang Schubert's "Ave Maria" at the White House at a state dinner for King George VI and Queen Elizabeth, and she would sing at the inauguration of President John F. Kennedy in 1961. In Eleanor's view, black people ought not to be denied the same privileges as white people. She gave her support to the civil rights movement, and struck up a friendship with Mary McLeod Bethune, an African American teacher and professor whom President Roosevelt appointed director of the Division of Negro Affairs of the National Youth Administration, part of the Works Progress Administration, in 1936. When Bethune came to the White House, Eleanor met her at the gate, embraced her, and walked arm in arm with her to avoid questions from the staff. In time, rumors spread about the "Eleanor Clubs" formed by servants to oppose their employers. Eleanor believed she had a moral duty to initiate changes that ensured racial equality.

Meanwhile, Franklin did not address racial problems, mainly for political reasons. He could not afford to lose the southern vote or the support of conservative southern Democrats in Congress.

CHAPTER 16

Eleanor and Joseph Lash

Every woman in public life has to develop skin
as tough as a rhinoceros hide.
—Eleanor Roosevelt

I n November 1939, Eleanor first met Joseph Lash, who had returned to New York after fighting the fascists during the Spanish Civil War. A 1931 graduate of City College in New York, Lash then earned a master's degree in philosophy and literature at Columbia University. He joined the Socialist Party of America and became an officer of the Student League for International Democracy. In addition he was executive secretary of the American Student Union and advocated for radical social change. He organized antiwar demonstrations on college campuses and wrote leftist pieces for the campus newspaper. A trim, neatly dressed man who brushed his dark, curly hair straight back from his forehead, Joe Lash had a strong, open face and prominent ears, and favored wearing a vest under his suit jacket.

Lash had been born in 1909, the oldest child of a Russian immigrant family. His father died when Joe was nine years old, and Joe's mother worked fifteen-hour days in their Harlem grocery store to feed her five children. Lash's son, Jonathan, who became president of Hampshire College from 2011 to 2018 and president of the World Resources Institute, said in an interview that his father had to leave school early to help run the family's grocery store during the 1918 flu epidemic. Joe worked hard all his life and was alienated from his Jewish faith, said Jonathan. "I found after he died he wanted me to read the Kaddish over his grave. He was conflicted—embarrassed to be Jewish."

In 1937 Lash resigned from the Socialist Party and described himself as a "full-time revolutionary," dedicated to fighting fascism and achieving the goals of international socialism. He immersed himself in these large causes. On August 23, 1939, Germany and the Soviet Union signed a nonaggression pact, which shocked the world, given the fact that the two leaders had radically different ideologies. The Hitler-Stalin decision frightened Lash, prompted his resignation as executive secretary of the American Student Union, and presaged the end of his idealism.

On November 30, 1939, Lash was subpoenaed to appear before the House Un-American Activities Committee (HUAC) and its conservative chairman, Martin Dies of Texas. Dies had been instructed by J. Edgar Hoover to carefully manage Lash, and he ordered a manhunt for Nazi sympathizers in New York. HUAC coordinated with Hoover on his hunt for subversives all over the United States. Lash was on Hoover's list, as was Eleanor. Before the committee hearings began, Eleanor asked FDR if he would mind if she showed up unannounced at Dies's committee to hear what Lash had to say. FDR agreed that she should go.

On the day of the hearing, December 1, Eleanor's arrival was a surprise to the members of the committee, including Chairman Dies. They invited her to sit with them, and she politely refused and sat instead with students watching the proceedings. To pass the time, she had brought her knitting basket. The sounds of her clicking needles—knit, purl, knit, knit, purl—could be heard throughout the room. Dies pressed Lash to name the Communists who were members of the American Student Union, but Lash refused. Instead, he ridiculed Dies by breaking into a song. "If you see an Un-American lurking far or near," sang Lash. "Just *alcoholize* with Martin Dies and he will disappear!" The audience erupted in laughter. Eleanor moved close to where students sat at the front of the committee room, and put down her knitting.

Eleanor was later told by Lash that he was terrified by the Nazi-Soviet pact, and to make up for it he tried to turn everything that day into a joke. That made sense to Eleanor, who, like many of her liberal friends in the Village, was also suspicious of the Soviet Union's intentions. Eleanor's presence that day changed the tone of Dies and the other committee members. They decided to treat Lash with more respect.

At the lunch hour a three-hour recess occurred. Eleanor invited Lash to come to the White House and bring the youth leaders with him. They were ten poorly dressed young people who had no money and carried shabby bags, and they were suddenly at the White House as lunch guests with the president and the first lady. Both FDR and Eleanor thought the House Un-American Activities Committee was not only unfair but sordid. Eleanor believed that the committee was trying to portray Lash as a Soviet spy. After lunch FDR excused himself to return to his office, and Eleanor and the students adjourned to her sitting room. There they said that they had supported FDR but were dismayed at his lack of attention to domestic issues. For example, they asked Eleanor, what about the rights of Negroes? What about the interests of American workers? Eleanor explained the challenges FDR had to face when he brought legislation to Congress, but the students had their own ideas. They wanted a Socialist Party separate from the traditional Democratic Party to put pressure on the government.

Eleanor and Lash soon became friends. Some weeks later, she entertained him at her small apartment on East 11th Street in the Village. A one-hour political discussion took place that evening. Lash told Eleanor that he had previously felt that America should remain neutral in the European struggle. His views had changed, however, and he understood now that the United States could not take a backseat to the unfolding events overseas. Eleanor paid attention to Joe Lash and treated him with respect. She invited him to spend time by himself at the Roosevelt family estate in Hyde Park. He was also invited to come to

Val-Kill. Eleanor enjoyed the time she spent with Lash. She liked his socialist ideas and was moved by Joe's stories of his difficult childhood.

Eleanor continued to talk politics with Lash and his friends, one of whom was Trude Pratt, also an activist, who had come to the United States in the early twenties from Germany. Trude and Joe had fallen in love. She was a married woman with three children and constantly worried that her husband in Germany would take the children away from her. Eleanor welcomed her to her homes at Val-Kill and in the Village. Though the Secret Service was concerned about Joe, they were particularly worried about Trude, because she was a militant from Germany. FDR liked Joe but was especially fond of Trude.

J. Edgar Hoover had been authorized by FDR to tell his agents to monitor people like Eleanor's every movement, and to tap her telephone without a warrant or her knowledge. This marked a reversal of a previous Justice Department edict that it would no longer permit investigations of government personnel outside the department. Hoover believed Eleanor was a troublemaker and probably a Communist.

In February 1943, Joe Lash was stationed in the air force at Chanute Field, in Illinois, to train as a weather eyewitness. He knew he was being watched by army intelligence and in fact noticed shortly after his arrival that items in his footlocker had been rearranged. He was not personally worried about this close observation, but he did not want to be an embarrassment for Eleanor.

His training at Chanute Field lasted three months. Eleanor and her private secretary, Malvina "Tommy" Thompson, stayed in a hotel in Urbana, Illinois, the closest city to the airfield, on March 4, 1943. An FBI informant reported that Eleanor ordered dinner for three people to be sent to her room. Lash checked into the room next to Eleanor and Tommy. Other meals were also served in their rooms. Sometimes they had lunch at the hotel dining room. Eleanor checked out of the hotel on March 7, 1943, at 7:35 a.m., and Lash departed just before her.

Their rooms were adjacent, room 330 for Lash and 332 for Eleanor and Tommy; both rooms were bugged and under surveillance. Two weeks later Joe again checked into the hotel, along with his future wife, Trude Pratt, taking room 332. Eleanor was not there. According to the FBI observer, the couple had sexual relations multiple times over that weekend. Hoover and the FBI purposely conflated the two women so that they could say Eleanor was having an affair with Lash. The only other evidence was letters that Joe and Eleanor exchanged and that the FBI opened as often as possible.

Yet Hoover continued to assert that Eleanor and Lash had engaged in sex, and he told Franklin and Harry Hopkins that the two were lovers. Nothing could have been farther from the truth. If anything, Eleanor was a mother figure to Lash; they would go on to enjoy a long friendship, and in time Lash helped write many of Eleanor's books. In an interview with *Publishers Weekly* in 1984, Lash said he believed that FBI agents wanted to prove they were lovers. "There wasn't any such relationship," he said. "It's an absurd accusation." He died on August 22, 1987, shortly after that interview.

Lash's wife, Trude, was close to Eleanor, and the two of them worked together to organize liberal organizations. Trude and Joe ultimately moved to Greenwich Village. "By the time I was old enough, I thought Mrs. Roosevelt was the greatest lady in the world," said their son Jonathan. "One New Year's Eve she stayed home and babysat for me. She asked me if I would like to read some books. I said yes. Then she asked if I said my prayers at night and she could see that I was embarrassed. She was very caring. The truth is, even now I say my prayers at night."

David Roosevelt, Eleanor's grandson, lives in Hyde Park. In an interview David said that Hoover worked hard to bring down his grandmother. "The longer Hoover saw who my grandmother was, the more she built her power base." For many years David has asked the FBI to release all the pages in Eleanor's case files. The file, numbered 62-62753, has nearly four thousand pages. About four hundred pages are about Eleanor's relationship with Lash. In all these years, the files have never been released. David believes that Hoover left instructions for his secretary to destroy the files. "I think we should get this whole thing declassified," said David Roosevelt. "What files were kept? I know the private files on Joe Lash were kept," he said. "And there were many attempts (fifteen, in fact) on my grandmother's life. Why aren't they in the files? What did Hoover have to do with that?"

Nonetheless Eleanor's files are a resource that has not given up all of its secrets. Chris Brick, an Eleanor scholar at George Washington University, submitted a Freedom of Information Act request in 2013 for information in Eleanor's files. The FOIA gave Brick most of the files, and one year later they released another 358 pages. However, twelve pages have not been released. In time, Brick filed a lawsuit in conjunction with Ralph Nader and the Public Litigation Group. On February 22, 2019, the judge in the case sided with the FBI and denied the petition to release the remaining twelve pages. Which raises the question: What is in those twelve pages that cannot be released?

CHAPTER 17

J. Edgar Hoover
Takes on Eleanor

Remember always that you not only have the right
to be an individual, you have an obligation.
—*Eleanor Roosevelt*

E ven though Eleanor was the first lady of the United
States, Hoover continued to investigate her and her
friends. In 1941, Eleanor found out that the FBI was investigating Edith B. Helm, who had been her social secretary for a dozen years. Eleanor complained to Franklin, to
Hoover, and to the attorney general, Robert Houghwout
Jackson. Hoover claimed he was unaware of "the identity
of Edith B. Helm or the fact that she was acting in a secre-
tarial capacity for you." Had the FBI known, Hoover told
both Eleanor and Franklin, "that inquiry would not have
been initiated."

Eleanor learned that FBI agents were also question-
ing and following Tommy Thompson. Again Eleanor protested to the president, the attorney general, and Hoover.

Two days later Eleanor wrote to Hoover: "I am surprised to learn that someone had been making inquiries about Miss Thompson at her apartment, asking neighborhood people if she comes and goes, how much company she has etc. This type of investigation seems to smack too much of the Gestapo methods . . . I cannot help resenting deeply the action in these two cases and if you have done this type of investigation of other people, I do not wonder that we are beginning to get an extremely jittery population." Almost no one challenged Hoover in such a manner, as his position was considered invulnerable. For her candor Eleanor made an enemy of Hoover for life.

Interestingly enough, FDR had a hand in Hoover's investigation of Eleanor. In August 1936, Hoover had come to the White House for a private meeting with the president. FDR told Hoover he wanted a "broad picture" of subversives in the United States. The next day Hoover and FDR met with Secretary of State Cordell Hull, who gave his enthusiastic support for the program. By year's end, Hoover had constructed a large bureaucratic empire. FDR's directive also allowed Hoover unlimited public resources to spy on his own personal enemies, which included the president's wife.

Eleanor continued to call Hoover out as often as possible. As Allida M. Black wrote in her book *Casting Her Own Shadow: Eleanor Roosevelt and the Shaping of Postwar Liberalism*, "Of all the controversial people and policies Eleanor Roosevelt promoted throughout her life, none generated a response equal to that provoked by her support of civil rights policies at home and abroad." Eleanor urged the black minority to continue their drive for freedom. As early as 1935, Eleanor had worked closely with her friend Mary McLeod Bethune, a civil rights leader, and the two women, one black, the other white, became friends. Hoover could not abide Eleanor's efforts and suggested that perhaps Eleanor herself had "Negro blood" in her veins.

From 1933 until 1962 Eleanor drove without Secret Service cover. In those years, she documented the aforementioned fifteen assassination attempts on her life. When she went to African American churches in the South to speak, dynamite was found wrapped around the tires on her car. In 1950, the Ku Klux Klan put a $25,000 bounty on Mrs. Roosevelt. Yet she persisted.

In the 1940s, a conservative newspaper columnist, Westbrook Pegler, a confidant of Hoover's, accused Eleanor of "commercializing her office as wife of the President and forfeiting the respect people are accustomed to giving one of her position." A 1993 article in *American Heritage* magazine said, "Eleanor Roosevelt's mere existence drove conservatives like Westbrook Pegler into spasms of rage." She tried to take the high road. In 1933, when the Scripps-Howard newspaper chain offered Pegler a syndicated daily column and he used it to express how much he despised most of the things Eleanor held dear, she used her own newspaper column, "My Day," to fight back in her own subtle way. In one 1942 column she sarcastically referred to the "virtuous Westbrook Pegler" who had opposed the New Deal.

In 1942, Eleanor and Franklin signed a four-year lease on a seven-room penthouse apartment in Manhattan, 15-A at 29 Washington Square West. The penthouse provided a grand view of much of the Village, and they planned to use it as their New York residence when World War II ended. As it happened, President Roosevelt never slept there.

The apartment was one floor above Tommy Thompson. Eleanor's secretary was born in the Bronx to working-class parents. She was short and stocky and spoke with a husky voice, and Eleanor had a nickname for her: "The Brick." For the rest of her life Eleanor would lean on Tommy—as a helper and a friend. Thompson was married and had a child, but she went everywhere with Eleanor. She helped her write her daily newspaper column, including correcting her spelling, and booked guests for her radio show. Eleanor and Tommy often walked Fala, the president's Scottish terrier, across Washington Square Park. (The small dog was much loved by the American public. MGM even made a newsreel of a day in the life of Fala.)

Not long after Eleanor and Franklin bought the penthouse apartment overlooking the famous square, two FBI agents showed up at the apartment of Angela Calomiris, a young photographer in the Village, and a lesbian friend of

Lape and Read. Angela had occasionally acted as an errand girl for Eleanor and Lape during the 1930s. She took mail to the post office and answered the phone at the East 11th Street apartments.

The FBI recruited Angela as an informant in search of information about the American Communist Party. She lived in an apartment on Jane Street, and then on Horatio Street, and finally in an apartment in a brownstone on West 12th Street. Whether she also spied on Eleanor for J. Edgar Hoover is unclear, but Angela did successfully infiltrate Communist leaders in the Village who were later sent to prison for conspiracy to advocate the overthrow of the government. Lisa Davis, a writer who currently lives in Greenwich Village, wrote a book about Angela and some of her friends, *Undercover Girl: The Lesbian Informant Who Helped the FBI Bring Down the Communist Party*.

From the files, it is clear that although Hoover couldn't prove Eleanor was a Communist herself, he believed that the fact many of her acquaintances were Communists was proof enough that she was as well.

CHAPTER 18

The Death of the President

*I think I lived those years very impersonally. It was almost
as if I had erected someone outside myself who was the president's
wife. I was lost somewhere deep inside myself. That is the way
I felt and worked until I left the White House.*
—Eleanor Roosevelt

In 1944, FDR prepared for his fourth run for the presidency in what would be the last full year of World War II. Eleanor was also in favor of another term. (Not until the ratification of the Twenty-Second Amendment in 1951 was there a constitutional limit of no more than two terms as president of the United States.) In March 1944 FDR had an examination by his doctors, who told him he had a heart ailment, high blood pressure, and bronchitis. Nonetheless, FDR won his unprecedented fourth term. World War II had him under immense strain, yet he led the free world to victory. Berlin was about to fall. Japan would surrender in the summer of 1945.

The war years of the 1940s in the Village had given rise to a renaissance, a time when, following the decade of the Depression, World War II made New York the capital of the Western world. Eleanor's days and nights there were rich and full. The writers, artists, and misfits in the Village lived alongside GIs home from the war who had gained more liberal attitudes about looser lifestyles in America. Anatole Broyard, who moved to the Village in 1946, would write in his memoir, *Kafka Was the Rage*, "The war had broken the rhythm of American life, and when we tried to pick it up again, we couldn't find it—it wasn't there."

The afternoon of April 12, 1945, Eleanor was not in the Village. She was in Washington making preparations for the charter meeting of the United Nations, a cause she had promoted strongly, that would take place in San Francisco in June. Franklin was in Warm Springs. Across the room Eleanor saw Tommy, who seemed to be out of breath, and who urgently asked Eleanor to answer the telephone. On the other end of the line her press secretary, Steve Early, told Eleanor that Franklin had collapsed. Early and Tommy advised her to travel to Warm Springs that very evening. Eleanor then learned that Dr. Howard Bruenn, a naval physician, had already been summoned to Warm Springs. When he arrived, he determined that the president had suffered a cerebral hemorrhage. At three-thirty, President Roosevelt's breathing stopped. "In my heart of hearts I knew what had happened, but one does not actually formulate these terrible thoughts until they are spoken," Eleanor later wrote.

She sent for Vice President Harry Truman. He arrived

at five-thirty without knowing why he had been summoned to the White House. He was sent to Eleanor's sitting room. Truman later remembered that Eleanor's dress was dark black and she looked exhausted. Eleanor stood and placed her arm on Truman's shoulder. Truman was FDR's third vice president and had not had much contact with him. "Harry," she said, "the President is dead." Truman could not speak. "Is there anything I can do for you?" asked Eleanor. "For you are in trouble now."

Truman was quickly sworn in as president. Eleanor asked to use the government airplane so she could get to Warm Springs quickly. Truman said yes, and Eleanor got into the plane, silent and alone.

The press wanted to know if the president was alive. Eleanor wanted no secrets. She told them the truth: Franklin had "slipped away." She was silent for a while and then said: "I am more sorry for the people of the country and of the world than I am for ourselves." Her responsibilities were now to the people.

In England the people were as shocked as the Americans. Winston Churchill addressed the House of Commons in a choked-up voice. "In Franklin Roosevelt there died the greatest friend we have ever known, and the greatest champion of freedom who has ever brought help and comfort from the New World to the Old."

At the time of his death at age sixty-three, Eleanor and Franklin had been married for forty years. Even though their marriage was not the usual romance, each had played a large role in the other's life, working together especially during the war years. In those times, Franklin Roosevelt exercised strong leadership to win World War II, and became one of the towering figures of the twentieth century. Meanwhile, Eleanor had her own ideas and circled around the New Deal at home with her desire to be a strong voice for liberalism, working to help civil rights leaders, labor leaders, and liberal spokesmen. She was earnest and determined to get things done. Franklin, often tired during the war years, said a prayer many times, "Dear God, please make Eleanor a little tired."

It was midnight when Eleanor arrived in Warm Springs, and she worked hard to be calm and composed. She embraced Franklin's cousins, Laura Delano and Margaret Suckley, as well as Grace Tully, then secretary to FDR. Everyone wanted to explain where they had been when the president died. Tully had just dressed for lunch when she heard that FDR was sick. Margaret had been sitting on the sofa crocheting when the president slumped forward in his chair. Then came the news Eleanor dreaded, from Laura. Lucy Mercer Rutherfurd, now a widow, had been in Warm Springs, visiting as Franklin sat for a portrait.

It had taken Eleanor a long time to get over her husband's affair with Lucy Mercer, her own former social secretary. Eleanor's daughter, Anna, had idolized Lucy over her own mother. Now in 1945, FDR had died at Warm Springs with Lucy near. Eleanor had hoped that Lucy's love for Franklin was behind her, but it was not. Laura

Delano told Eleanor that Lucy had been to the White House several times when Eleanor was not there. Anna had been present as hostess at these times, without telling her mother. Eleanor realized she had been deceived by her husband and daughter. After hearing Laura's story, she went into the room where Franklin lay and closed the door. She remained inside for five minutes. "When she came out her eyes were dry again, her face grave but composed," wrote Grace Tully.

Franklin Roosevelt had always lived a charmed life. He had parents who loved him and sent him to the best schools. When he contracted polio, he was certain that he would walk again. He had a magic way about him when he spoke, carrying a big confident smile, and he had the ability to tell Americans that, having gone through the Great Depression as well as World War II, they were much stronger now. However, the emotional parts of his life had remained highly secret. He wanted to marry Lucy Mercer, but his mother forbade it. Franklin had secretly brought Lucy to Warm Springs in his last days and she stayed until he died. Three years later, on July 31, 1948, Lucy would die herself of leukemia at the age of fifty-seven.

It was up to Eleanor to prepare for Franklin's funeral. She went to his bedroom to find clothes for his burial—a white shirt, a double-breasted blue business suit. She stood behind him and his body when he was brought into the living room and placed in a casket. The following morning thousands of people in Warm Springs went to the railroad station to say goodbye to their president. A military guard lifted the coffin into the back car of FDR's train.

As the funeral train moved north toward Washington, Eleanor was alone for most of the journey. Hundreds of people lined the track. Eleanor had made sure that a special cradle was erected that held the casket up to the height of the windows so that it could be seen by the public all along the way. As Doris Kearns Goodwin wrote in *No Ordinary Time*, "Men stood with their arms around the shoulders of wives and mothers. . . . Men and women openly wept. Church choirs gathered at the trackside and sang 'Rock of Ages' and 'Abide with Me.' As the train made its way through Georgia's valleys and hills . . . four Negro women in a cotton field working on a spring planting were kneeling near the edge of the field. Their hands were clasped together in prayerful supplication."

The train arrived in Washington, D.C., on April 14, at 10 a.m. The casket was transferred to a black caisson with six white horses. It made its way down Pennsylvania Avenue in the rain as five hundred thousand mourners lined the streets. On arriving at the White House, FDR's coffin was lifted high and carried up the front steps. Eleanor asked for a few minutes alone with her husband in the East Room. "Please don't let anyone else come in," she asked of J. B. West, the White House usher. Eleanor stood at the casket, West later said, gazing down into her husband's face. Then she took a gold ring from her finger and placed it on the president's hand.

A few days later, when Eleanor returned to the White House for a small service, the East Room was filled with red flowers. The Roosevelt family sat in the front row, across the aisle from President Truman and his wife. Behind the Roosevelt family members sat cabinet members, Supreme Court justices, labor leaders, and diplomats from all the countries of the (soon to be) United Nations.

Eleanor asked that the ceremony begin with "Faith of Our Fathers" and close with Roosevelt's first inaugural quotation: "The only thing we have to fear is fear itself." She worked hard to remain calm. When everyone left, Secret Service agent Milton Lipson recalled, "Mrs. Roosevelt took a last look at all the flowers and asked us if we'd arrange to have them taken to a mental hospital." Eleanor wept, and added, "Of course, if any of you wanted a souvenir, please help yourself."

Later that evening, another funeral train headed toward Hyde Park along the east bank of the Hudson. In her book *This I Remember*, Eleanor wrote, "I lay in my berth with the window shade up, looking out at the countryside that he had loved and watching the faces of the people at stations, and even at the crossroads, who came to pay their last tribute all through the night. The only recollection I clearly have is thinking about 'The Lonesome Train,' the musical poem about Lincoln's death. ["A lonesome train on a lonesome track / Seven coaches painted black / A slow train, a quiet train / Carrying Lincoln home again . . ."] I had always liked it so well—and now this was so much like it."

After the train arrived at dawn in Hyde Park, the funeral cortege, with the caisson and six horses, made its way up the hill, led by the Marines and the West Point cadet band. Directly behind the cortege walked a hooded horse with an empty saddle and its stirrups reversed—the traditional symbol of a fallen leader. The service was held in a rectangular garden, the walls lined by West Point cadets. Reverend George Anthony, Franklin's seventy-eight-year-old pastor, quoted the familiar lines: "We commit his body to the ground, earth to earth, dust to dust." West Point cadets gave FDR a twenty-one-gun salute. As the crowd dispersed, Eleanor remained in the garden and in a short time she quietly walked away.

After FDR's state funeral on April 14, 1945, Tommy started packing Eleanor's clothes, books, and other possessions in the White House in preparation for moving to her new apartment on Washington Square in the Village. That weekend Lorena Hickok was going to join them at the apartment. Eleanor sent a note to Hick: "The Trumans have been to lunch and nearly all that I can do is done. The upstairs looks desolate and I will be glad to leave tomorrow. It is empty and without purpose and now in its wake those of us who lay in his shadow have to start again under our own momentum and wonder what we can achieve. I may be weary when we get home tomorrow but I am so glad you will be at the apartment."

CHAPTER 19

Without Franklin

You have to accept whatever comes and
the only important thing is that you meet it with courage
and with the best that you have to give.
—*Eleanor Roosevelt*

The penthouse apartment that overlooked Washington Square Park had a wheelchair-accessible lobby. It was one of the reasons she and FDR had chosen to lease the place. But now he was gone, and it was Eleanor, a born and bred New Yorker, who would live there until 1949.

Tommy continued to work for Eleanor until 1953, when she died at sixty-one from a brain tumor. During her lifetime, Tommy was either in the Village, the White House, or at Val-Kill, helping Eleanor when she needed her. Tommy's niece, Ellie Zartman, who now lives in Washington, spent her summers playing with many other children at Val-Kill. In an interview she said, "One time Mrs. Roosevelt had a hot dog picnic at Val-Kill for us and every night we would go into Mrs. Roosevelt's living room and she read stories to all the children. I loved the stories, but I was a wiggle kid, knee to knee."

David Roosevelt, a grandson of Eleanor, remembers sleeping on the porch with his grandmother at the apartment on Washington Square and spending time with her in the Village. Hick remained friends with Tommy and Eleanor for many years. She lived at the White House and then moved to Val-Kill cottage, where she lived until her death in 1968, at the age of seventy-five. Nancy and Marion had always been jealous of Hick and Eleanor's friendship, and Eleanor bought out their share of Val-Kill. The truth was Eleanor had outgrown the two of them. Nancy died on August 16, 1962, and Marion died on May 16, 1983.

It was Esther Lape, journalist and organizer, who made the first efforts to fight for a system of comprehensive healthcare in the United States. The American Medical Association refused to consider it, and opposed President Harry S. Truman's proposal for national health insurance. In the 1950s, Lape and Eleanor attempted to upgrade medical healthcare for all. President Dwight D. Eisenhower told them he liked the idea, but the AMA lobby, concerned about doctors losing autonomy to the federal government, blocked their goal then, as it has blocked similar efforts since.

In 1993, Hillary Rodham Clinton led a task force to provide comprehensive healthcare plans that would have required each American to have health insurance. Her medical plan never came to a vote in the House or the Senate. Hillary had always been inspired by Eleanor and knew that it had been the goal of FDR to create a healthcare system guaranteed for all people. (Truman, too, believed Roosevelt would have wanted it.) Hillary and Eleanor had many things in common: they made their voices heard in their difficult marriages, and they believed that the government had a responsibility to the citizens. When it came to medical health issues, however, it was Lape who pressed for a better system of healthcare. All these years later, we continue to wrestle with many of the problems that FDR and Eleanor wanted to fix, including universal healthcare.

Joe Lash once asked Esther Lape whether Eleanor was ever in love with Franklin. And, if so, was she still in love with him? "I don't think she ever stopped loving him," said Lape. Then she quoted "A Woman's Shortcomings," the poem by Elizabeth Barrett Browning that Franklin used when he asked Eleanor to marry him:

> *Unless you can think when the song is done,*
> *No other is soft in the rhythm;*
> *Unless you can feel, when left by One,*
> *That all men else go with him;*
> *Unless you can know, when upraised by his breath*
> *That your beauty itself wants proving;*
> *Unless you can swear, "For life, for death!"—*
> *Oh, fear to call it loving!*

Eleanor never forgot the morning in 1921 when Franklin woke up unable to move his legs. His illness thrust

Eleanor into the spotlight, as she became Franklin's proxy on the road. It was an unprecedented role for a first lady—or any woman—at that time. During her initial year as first lady, Eleanor traveled thirty-eight thousand miles on inspection trips around the country. The following year's total was forty-two thousand miles. After that, reporters stopped counting.

As a result of contracting polio, FDR met many men, women, and children with the disease, and he worked and exercised alongside many of them at Warm Springs. (This experience was behind the president's support of the founding of the National Foundation for Infantile Paralysis in 1938 and its famous "March of Dimes" fund-raising drives.)

By the time he contracted polio, their relationship had become Edwardian—Franklin had his court and Eleanor had hers. It was as if they could see themselves as they really were, no more arguments. A part of Eleanor would always think of Franklin and feel "inadequate," fearing there was no longer "any fundamental love to draw on, just respect and affection." But Eleanor gave him hope he drew upon to lead the country, and during the war years Franklin sent her all over the globe to visit American troops. Though she could be angry with him, it is fair to say that Eleanor probably never stopped loving him. "My husband and I came through the years with an acceptance of each other's faults and foibles, a deep understanding, warm affection and agreement on essential values. We depended on each other."

A widow at sixty years old, Eleanor did not know what to do with herself, a predicament shared by many women who had lost their husbands in World War II. Few women in the country garnered more respect than Eleanor. Joe Lash and many others pleaded with her to run for president, governor, or senator. However, Eleanor did not believe in her time that any woman would be president. It was Esther Lape who advised her to take the time to consider what were "the tremendously increased powers that are so peculiarly now yours."

The Franklin D. Roosevelt Presidential Library opened on June 30, 1941, while he was still in office. It set a precedent for future presidential libraries. Before his death, President Roosevelt told Eleanor that she should turn over the big house at Hyde Park to the federal government as a museum. This bequest was also written into his will. Eleanor spent several months arranging for the transfer. The Museum opened to the public on April 12, 1946, exactly one year after President Roosevelt's death. The Library celebrated its seventy-fifth anniversary in 2016.

Eleanor was appointed by President Truman to be the US representative to the United Nations Commission on Human Rights and became a leading force behind the UN's Declaration on Human Rights, adopted in 1948, and a strong leader in New York politics.

The 1930s through the 1940s were the zenith of the power of Robert Moses, New York's "master builder" of public works who came to favor highway projects over public transportation, but by the late fifties his influence was not what it used to be. Despite never being elected to public office, he once held twelve job titles simultaneously and wielded extraordinary power in shaping New York City and environs. A brilliant, headstrong person, he had been in power so long that as a young man in the 1920s he tangled with Governor Franklin Roosevelt over the diversion of funds meant to build a parkway through the Hudson Valley. Moses believed that New York City's survival depended on slowing white flight to the suburbs by making the city's core borough, Manhattan, a more attractive place.

In 1959, he submitted plans to build the LOMEX, or Lower Manhattan Expressway, which would mean the construction of a ten-lane highway cutting through lower Manhattan. To do that Moses decided to drive a Fifth Avenue extension straight through Washington Square, dividing the park into two isolated strips. Eleanor was aware of what was going on. Villagers refused to give up the square and insisted it be maintained as a large park. Moses called that "an absurdity," "completely unworkable." The famous community activist Jane Jacobs formed an opposition group and recruited Eleanor as a member, in addition to Margaret Mead, journalist William Whyte, and historian Lewis Mumford. Eleanor personally led a delegation to City Hall to support closing the square to all traffic. In 1959 Moses's plan was finally abandoned, and today Washington Square Park, still the heart of Greenwich Village, remains closed to all traffic.

CHAPTER 20

Eleanor and
John F. Kennedy

It isn't enough to talk about peace. One must believe in it.
It isn't enough to believe in it. One must work at it.
—*Eleanor Roosevelt*

During the 1950s Eleanor remained politically active by advising Harry Truman, Adlai Stevenson, and eventually the young Massachusetts senator John F. Kennedy. All her work was behind the scenes, but without her backing a Democrat running for high office was bound to lose. Stevenson, governor of Illinois, was the Democratic nominee for president in 1952. Eleanor enthusiastically supported him though she understood there was little hope he could win against Dwight Eisenhower.

The Democrats had held the office for twenty years. The country was in the midst of the "Red Scare" of the 1950s that included the anticommunist diatribes of Wisconsin senator Joseph R. McCarthy, who claimed the State Department and even the Army were riddled with "reds";

183

continuing investigations by the House Committee on Un-American Activities (especially of former State Department official Alger Hiss); and loyalty oaths, mass firings, and imprisonments, often upon the mere suspicion of communist sympathies. The red scare of the 1950s had been fueled in part by the stories of the Hollywood Ten in 1947—directors and screenwriters who refused to testify to HUAC about their own or colleagues' current or former membership in the Communist Party and were blacklisted as a result, stories that appeared on the front page of almost every American newspaper. An atmosphere of fear and accusation surrounded the hearings being broadcast on television and inhibited free speech in America. This marked the beginning of what many referred to as hard-line Republicanism, personified by McCarthy and an ambitious congressman, senator, and vice president named Richard M. Nixon.

In 1956 Eleanor again supported Stevenson. After four years of Eisenhower, she was ready for a change. She must have known that Stevenson had little chance of winning. The country's postwar economy was prospering and the Cold War was going strong, along with the arms race. Despite Eleanor's efforts, Eisenhower won a second term.

In 1960 she encouraged Adlai Stevenson to run a third time. However, Stevenson by then was viewed as a loser. Eleanor attended the Democratic National Convention and addressed the delegates. The choice at the July convention was between Senate Majority Leader Lyndon Johnson of Texas and John F. Kennedy. Kennedy won the nomination.

Eleanor, often called the mother of the Democratic Party, gave him only a halfhearted endorsement.

After he won the nomination, Kennedy realized he had to ask for Eleanor's support. She told him not to worry about her. If Kennedy wanted to talk, Eleanor suggested he talk to her sons and not her. The fact was that Eleanor did not believe that Kennedy was old enough to be president. In the 1950s, he had served as senator from Massachusetts during the time that Senator McCarthy effectively took over the Senate. Eleanor had challenged him then to be more outspoken in his opposition to McCarthyism. Kennedy watched McCarthy frighten everyone into silence for fear of appearing to be soft on Communism. It would still be a delicate line for Kennedy to walk, even though McCarthy had been censured by the Senate in 1954 and had died in disgrace in 1957.

Eleanor told Kennedy she would not go against him, but he could not count on her to campaign for him. She did not trust JFK's father, Joseph P. Kennedy, who had made a large fortune in the stock market and had served as FDR's first chairman of the Securities and Exchange Commission. Moreover, the Kennedy family was Catholic, and Eleanor did not believe a Catholic could win the election. She had even been branded anti-Catholic, when in July 1949 she had experienced a significant disagreement with Cardinal Francis Spellman, the archbishop of New York, over federal funding for parochial schools.

This was a real problem for JFK. He knew he needed Eleanor's support and endorsement, and he arranged a meeting at Val-Kill, which took place in August of 1960. The two of them talked over lunch, with Eleanor seated in her usual rocking chair. According to Allida Black in her book *Casting Her Own Shadow: Eleanor Roosevelt and the Shaping of Postwar Liberalism*, "a firm but polite" Eleanor "was determined to leave her mark on John Kennedy, the last Democratic presidential aspirant with whom she expected to have contact, and determined but wary John Kennedy struggl[ed] to make a final appeal for support without tarnishing his own charisma." Eleanor told the press afterward that Kennedy was likely to make a good president if elected, and Kennedy ended up winning in a very close election. The eminent economist John Kenneth Galbraith later said he believed it was Eleanor's support that swayed the vote his way.

In a letter she wrote the day after their meeting, Eleanor said: "I have no promises from the Senator [Kennedy] but I have the distinct feeling that he is planning on working closely with Adlai. I also had the feeling that here was a man who could learn. I liked him better than I ever had before because he seemed so little cocksure, and I think he has a mind that is open to new ideas." She added her "final judgment that here is a man who wants to leave a record (perhaps for ambitious personal reasons as people say) but I rather think because he really is interested in helping the people of his own country and mankind in general. I will be surer of this as time goes on, but I think I am not mistaken in feeling that he would make a good President if elected."

CHAPTER 21

The First Feminist

People grow through experience if they meet life honestly
and courageously. This is how character is built.
—*Eleanor Roosevelt*

After Franklin's death, Eleanor decided she needed a doctor and asked Trude Lash for a recommendation. Trude recommended David Gurewitsch, who also was Trude's doctor. He soon became Eleanor's physician and trusted friend. His wife, Edna, wrote a book, *Kindred Souls*, published in 2002, about the years she and her husband, David, lived with Eleanor.

David and Eleanor found out that they had something in common: each of them was raised in a household without a father. David was the son of Russian-Jewish immigrant parents, and his father, a philosopher, died at twenty-six, three months before David was born, in 1902. His mother believed his father had committed suicide. She sent him and his brother to live with her parents in Russia. Over the next five years she studied medicine in England, and so David did not have any interaction with his mother for the first five years of his life. When she completed medical training, she started her practice in Berlin, and David and his brother joined her there.

David was a handsome, cultured, and at that time single man. He and Eleanor took trips together to Germany, Morocco, India, and Yugoslavia. In September 1957, they took a month-long trip to the Soviet Union. This occurred during the height of the Cold War, and Hoover's FBI agents followed along, transmitting copies of Eleanor's speeches and noting whom she met during the trip.

In David's mind, he and Eleanor were not lovers. She was sixty-three when they met and he was forty-five. Eleanor understood that younger, more beautiful women wanted to be with David, but with Franklin gone, she missed the talk about politics and friendship which she found with David. Her letters to him showed her affection for him.

> David my dearest—
>
> I've been sitting here thinking of you to-night and wondering why I make you shy. I want you to feel at home with me as you would with a member of your family and I can't achieve it! Something is wrong with me! I'd love to hear you call me by my first name but you can't. Perhaps it is my age! I do love you and you are always in my thoughts and if that bothers you I could hide it. I'm good at that. . . . In the meantime love me a little, and show it if you can and remember

to take care of yourself for you are the most precious person in the world.

In February 1958, David fell in love with Edna Perkel, a young, beautiful art dealer who primarily sought old master paintings and whom David had met at a performance of the Pirandello play *Six Characters in Search of an Author*. In time, David asked Edna to marry him. Eleanor was not pleased, but she had no reason to ask David to give up his marriage. She stayed formal with Edna and called her "Miss Perkel." She insisted that the wedding ceremony take place in her New York apartment. Edna was surprised and wrote a letter to Eleanor: "I know how much you mean to David and what your feelings and opinions mean to him. I can repay you only by doing all I can to make David happy."

Eleanor, Edna, and David moved into a townhouse at 55 East 74th Street in the fall of 1960. Eleanor lived downstairs and Edna and David lived upstairs and kept a watchful eye on Eleanor, who was now seventy-six years old. On November 8, 1960, election night, the front door of the house was open, as was the door to Eleanor's apartment. When she learned that John F. Kennedy had won the election, she was thrilled. She asked her friends that night to join her to celebrate his victory. By then Eleanor had come to respect Kennedy and was proud when he became president.

Eleanor took great care not to intrude on David and

Edna's lives. She always called before going up the stairs to their apartment. She did not want to duplicate the behavior of her own very intrusive mother-in-law.

In 1960 she was diagnosed with aplastic anemia, an incurable bone marrow disease. Yet she kept up her travels and public appearances. For instance, on February 15, 1960, she appeared on an ABC broadcast titled *The Frank Sinatra Timex Show*. Wearing a long dress with bows at her waist, Eleanor told Sinatra that "she was not a singer by any stretch, and could not dance." Sinatra asked her what her favorite word was that kept her going. Eleanor said, "The word is HOPE. It's the most neglected word in our language. Yet without hope, there can be no solution to mankind's trouble."

By November 1960 Eleanor was the most admired woman in the world. She had seen most of the countries on earth, including the Soviet Union, Morocco, Iran, Hong Kong, Indonesia, and Yugoslavia. She was particularly loved in India and Pakistan because of her strong stand in favor of racial equality in the United States. On all of her trips, she met with many leaders, but she mostly enjoyed her visits with ordinary people, especially with young children and their parents.

She was known all over the world as the woman who had lived in the White House longer than any other first lady. Her parallel in today's world is Michelle Obama, who, like Eleanor, has advanced the cause of freedom, peace, and justice for all lives without regard to color.

On November 7, 1962, Eleanor died at the house

on 55 East 74th Street, with David, Edna, and Eleanor's daughter, Anna, in the room. She had lost any strength she had left and her breath was short. She had just turned seventy-eight and no longer had the will to live. Before she died, Eleanor told Maureen Corr, her current secretary, what she wanted at her funeral: a plain pine casket, no flowers, and a simple service. Laura Delano, FDR's eccentric cousin, still managed to put a small bouquet under the casket, and no one disturbed it.

Hundreds of people of all races came to the funeral on November 10, 1962, at Hyde Park. Three presidents attended: Harry Truman, Dwight Eisenhower, and John F. Kennedy. Eleanor's casket was lowered next to Franklin's in the rose garden. Their graves are marked with a simple marble stone inscribed "Franklin Delano Roosevelt, 1882–1945 and Anna Eleanor Roosevelt, 1884–1962." They were not just man and wife but two distant Roosevelt cousins, who loved the "field of roses" and changed the world.

In the six decades since Eleanor's death, the Village has changed enormously, as has the city of New York, the country, the world. But then again, the Village in 1962, when Eleanor died, was much different from the Village of the 1920s. The Village has long been attractive to gay men, and its history now includes the famous Stonewall Riots that took place on Christopher Street beginning June 28,

1969, which is generally regarded as the start of the modern LGBT movement. The site and surrounding blocks were designated a US national monument in 2016.

A few years before Eleanor died, Norman Mailer, Edwin Fancher, and Dan Wolf founded *The Village Voice*, a weekly alternative newspaper that covered cultural, political, racial, and sexual issues from a decidedly liberal point of view. In its time *The Voice* won three Pulitzer Prizes and a George Polk Award, and featured the work of columnist Nat Hentoff (jazz and civil liberties) and art critic Robert Christgau, along with arty black-and-white photographs by Sylvia Plachy and Fred McDarrah. (*The Voice* was also popular in the 1990s for its racy personal ads, which by themselves constituted for readers a kind of thrilling anthropological window into the more unconventional sexual behaviors of New Yorkers.) The paper, alas, was subject to all the same economic pressures that threatened more conventional periodicals, but when at last it was shuttered in 2018, after sixty-three years of publication, it had made an enormous contribution to American culture. It also published investigative journalism, including articles by Wayne Barrett, a fearless *Voice* columnist who in four decades exposed many politicians and landlords, including Donald J. Trump, who at the time, 1979, was just a bombastic and ostensibly successful developer.

On March 8, 2017, a worldwide strike for women coincided with International Women's Day, and hundreds of women gathered in Washington Square Park, many dressed in red and carrying signs: "Racism Is For Profit," "My Body Is Not Your Business," "Honor Humanity," and other slogans of progressive protest. If the women had looked up, toward the apartment that Eleanor once lived in, she would have been pleased. It was just the kind of strike of which Eleanor approved.

Today, the neighborhood is not affordable for bohemians and misfits and struggling artists, who have largely decamped to less expensive neighborhoods in Brooklyn, Queens, or Hoboken. Affluent new residents have attracted expensive restaurants, and many of the mom-and-pop stores were forced to close. Bleecker, formerly a street of coffee shops and folk music clubs whose fame was spread by a Simon & Garfunkel song (misspelled as "Bleeker Street"), and Christopher Street, legendary as the heart of the gay community because of the Stonewall Inn at Sheridan Square, are now dotted with chic and trendy shops that bohemians cannot afford. New York University absorbs increasingly more buildings, including the penthouse where Eleanor lived. But there is still a vibe to the Village. On any day of the week, one can see performers with guitars and portable pianos out in the middle of Washington Square, along with artisans displaying their works, people playing chess, and students from New York University reading or meeting up with friends. The young flock to the park to see and be seen, and older citizens like to sit on the benches there to think and remember. Folks from other New York neighborhoods regularly come to walk or eat in the Village, especially during the spring and summer, knowing they will respond—as did Eleanor Roosevelt—to the crooked, charming streets, the intimate new restaurants, the brick townhouses, and the knowledge that there never has been and never will be any place else quite like it.

Acknowledgments

My deep appreciation goes first to my magnificent agent, Amy Hughes, and my amazing editor, Colin Harrison, who supported this book from the beginning, and through a pandemic, until it was completed. Everyone at Scribner and Simon & Schuster offered their support from home in a challenging work environment amid COVID-19, including Sarah Goldberg, Mark LaFlaur, and their staff. In addition, many thanks to Leah Caldwell, Cory Leahy, and Barbara Miller for their help with editing, wordcraft, and the technology to pass along suggestions. Drury Wellford, our photographic consultant, is one of a kind, providing photographs from files and archives that no one but Drury knows exist. The research was facilitated by interviews with David Roosevelt, Eleanor's grandson; Ellie Zartman, Malvina "Tommy" Thompson's niece; and Allida M. Black, author of *Casting Her Own Shadow: Eleanor Roosevelt and the Shaping of Postwar Liberalism.* I offer generous thanks to the staff at the New York Public Library and the Franklin D. Roosevelt Presidential Library and Museum. Many thanks to Calvin Trillin, esteemed journalist, author, and contribu-

ACKNOWLEDGMENTS

tor to *The New Yorker* since 1963 and longtime resident of Greenwich Village, for his insights into the Village.

Joanie Brooks, my closest friend, was a source of constant encouragement and an indispensable Information Technology coach in these COVID times.

To his surprise, my husband, Lucky Russell, became a continuing proofreader through each chapter.

Notes on Sources

Prologue

For the descriptions of the Vanderbilt Ball, I relied on a blog entry from the Museum of the City of New York, "Vanderbilt Ball—how a costume ball changed New York elite society," complete with photos of Mrs. Cornelius Vanderbilt III dressed as "Electric Light." The ball was the most anticipated party of the year, and all of New York's elite were desperate to attend. This was the high-society life that Eleanor's parents sought for her.

Chapter 1: New York, New York

For the chapter on Eleanor's birth and childhood, I depended on *Eleanor Roosevelt, Volume I: The Early Years, 1884–1933* by Blanche Wiesen Cook (1992) and *Roosevelt House at Hunter College: The Story of Franklin & Eleanor's New York City Home* by Deborah S. Gardner (2009).

NOTES ON SOURCES

Chapter 2: The Hard Years

By the age of ten, Eleanor's mother, sister, and father had died. To convey the hardship of this time, I relied on details from *Eleanor and Franklin* by Joseph P. Lash (1971), in particular his telling of Eleanor's May 1890 journey to Europe aboard the *Britannica*, which was rammed by a steamer on its first day at sea. (The first of two volumes that Lash published about the former first lady, *Eleanor and Franklin: The Story of Their Relationship, Based on Eleanor Roosevelt's Private Papers* [1971] won both the Pulitzer Prize for biography and the National Book Award for biography.)

Chapter 3: The Making of a Heroine

On Eleanor's early schooling and the development of her strong sense of self, Blanche Wiesen Cook's *Eleanor Roosevelt, Volume I: The Early Years, 1884–1933* (1992) and Joseph P. Lash's *Eleanor and Franklin* (1971) proved valuable sources.

Chapter 4: The Dream of Love

Eleanor's initial forays into the Village are described in Blanche Wiesen Cook's *Eleanor Roosevelt, Volume I: The Early Years, 1884–1933* (1992). For details on FDR's childhood, I relied on Geoffrey C. Ward's biography *A First-Class Temperament: The Emergence of Franklin Roosevelt, 1905–1928* (2014), and Sara Delano Roosevelt's memoir, *My Boy Franklin: As Told by Mrs. James Roosevelt to Isabel Leighton and Gabrielle Forbush*

(1933). Hazel Rowley's *Franklin and Eleanor: An Extraordinary Marriage* (2011) provided details on the couple's engagement.

Chapter 5: Wife and Mother

On Eleanor and Franklin's wedding day (and night), I relied on Joseph P. Lash (*Eleanor and Franklin* [1971]) and Hazel Rowley (*Franklin and Eleanor: An Extraordinary Marriage* [2011]), as well as *Mrs. L: Conversations with Alice Roosevelt Longworth* by Michael Teague (1981) and Eleanor's book *This Is My Story* (1950).

Chapter 6: Victorian Restraint, Upended

After Eleanor discovered Lucy Mercer's love letters to Franklin, she insisted he end the affair. Franklin complied, but mostly because divorce would have had an undesirable impact on his political career. This period would redefine the couple's marriage, allowing space for the two to live independent lives, as detailed in Doris Kearns Goodwin's *No Ordinary Time: Franklin & Eleanor Roosevelt: The Home Front in WWII* (1995). For other details on the early and turbulent years of Eleanor and Franklin's marriage, I've depended on Hazel Rowley's *Franklin and Eleanor: An Extraordinary Marriage* (2011).

Chapter 7: Bohemians and Prohibition in the Village

Village Voice editor Ross Wetzsteon's *Republic of Dreams: Greenwich Village: The American Bohemia* (2003) and John Strausbaugh's history of the area, *The Village: 400 Years of Beats and Bohemians, Radicals and Rogues: A History of Greenwich Village* (2014), provided information on the Village in the years immediately following the end of World War I. Before Eleanor's introduction to the Village, the area's reputation as a space for unconventionality and artistic experimentation was well established.

Chapter 8: Eleanor in Greenwich Village

The friendships Eleanor formed in the Village among the League of Women Voters helped her forge a life independent from her marriage, yet they also gave her the confidence that would eventually help lift Franklin to the presidency. On Eleanor's friendship with Esther Lape and Elizabeth Read, Hazel Rowley's *Franklin and Eleanor: An Extraordinary Marriage* (2011) and Blanche Wiesen Cook's *Eleanor Roosevelt, Volume I: The Early Years, 1884–1933* (1992) were essential sources.

Chapter 9: Polio Strikes

On Franklin's deteriorating health and Eleanor's assistance during this "trial by fire," Joseph P. Lash's *Eleanor and Franklin* (1971) provided useful context.

Chapter 10: Franklin and Eleanor, the Years Apart

Hazel Rowley's *Franklin and Eleanor: An Extraordinary Marriage* (2011) gave insight on how the couple's marriage became a professional and political collaboration as opposed to a traditional marriage. On the debate surrounding FDR's relationship with his secretary, "Missy," and whether or not it was sexual, Rowley, Blanche Wiesen Cook (*Eleanor Roosevelt, Volume I: The Early Years, 1884–1933* [1992]), and Doris Kearns Goodwin (*No Ordinary Time: Franklin & Eleanor Roosevelt: The Home Front in WWII* [1995]) all weighed in on the matter, with uncertain conclusions. Eleanor's activism against Teddy Roosevelt Jr.'s gubernatorial campaign is documented in Cook's *Volume I*.

Chapter 11: J. Edgar Hoover in the Village

Eleanor's FBI file, initially established due to her support for the World Court and the League of Nations, would eventually grow to 3,900 pages. To trace Hoover's monitoring of Eleanor and her friends in the Village, I relied on Curt Gentry's *J. Edgar Hoover: The Man and the Secrets* (2001). On Eleanor's frank manner with Hoover, I relied on a *Washington Post* article from June 1982 by Ted Gup.

Chapter 12: Finding Her Own Way

FDR took an active role in the construction and vision of the cottage at Val-Kill, sometimes to Eleanor's chagrin. Details of this vision, as a place with "an old-fashioned swimming hole" as opposed to "a beautiful marble bath," came from Blanche Wiesen Cook's *Eleanor Roosevelt, Volume I: The Early Years, 1884–1933* (1992). On Eleanor's time as a teacher at Todhunter

School, where she taught history and literature and took her students on field trips to New York to see tenements, I relied on Hazel Rowley (*Franklin and Eleanor: An Extraordinary Marriage* [2011]) and Cook.

Chapter 13: The Governor's Mansion

FDR and Eleanor's move to Albany and subsequent changes to Eleanor's life are documented in Joseph P. Lash's *Eleanor and Franklin* (1971) and Blanche Wiesen Cook's *Eleanor Roosevelt, Volume I: The Early Years, 1884–1933* (1992). During this period, FDR hired Earl Miller as Eleanor's bodyguard. The intimate bond between Miller and Eleanor is described in Cook's *Volume I* and Hazel Rowley's *Franklin and Eleanor: An Extraordinary Marriage* (2011).

Chapter 14: Eleanor Roosevelt's Erotic Relationship

Lorena Hickok's childhood, journalism career, and the onset of her erotic relationship with Eleanor are recounted in Susan Quinn's *Eleanor and Hick: The Love Affair That Shaped a First Lady* (2017). Excerpts from Hick's unfinished manuscript, describing her and Eleanor's relationship, are from Blanche Wiesen Cook's *Eleanor Roosevelt, Volume I: The Early Years, 1884–1933* (1992) and Hazel Rowley's *Franklin and Eleanor: An Extraordinary Marriage* (2011).

Chapter 15: Eleanor as First Lady

Eleanor did not quickly warm to the role of first lady, writing to Hick that her "zest in life" had faded, according to Doris Kearns Goodwin's *No Ordinary Time: Franklin & Eleanor Roosevelt: The Home Front in WWII* (1995). Her adjustment to life as first lady is covered in Blanche Wiesen Cook's *Eleanor Roosevelt, Volume II: The Defining Years, 1933–1938* (2000) as is Eleanor's work that led to the government funding the construction of the town of Arthurdale in West Virginia for the benefit of miners.

Chapter 16: Eleanor and Joseph Lash

When Joseph Lash was called to testify before the House Committee on Un-American Activities, Eleanor attended in person, knitting as the committee asked Lash to give the names of his Communist friends, as documented by Hazel Rowley (*Franklin and Eleanor: An Extraordinary Marriage* [2011]). Rowley's work describes the friendship that developed afterward between Lash and Eleanor, a friendship the FBI would closely monitor.

Chapter 17: J. Edgar Hoover Takes on Eleanor

Hoover's relentless tracking of Eleanor and her friends is covered by Curt Gentry in *J. Edgar Hoover: The Man and the Secrets* (2001).

Chapter 18: The Death of the President

On Eleanor's actions and grief following FDR's death, including her dismay at finding out that Lucy Mercer had continued to visit the White House, I've depended on Hazel Rowley (*Franklin and Eleanor: An Extraordinary Marriage* [2011]). The proceedings of FDR's funeral are covered by Doris Kearns Goodwin (*No Ordinary Time: Franklin & Eleanor Roosevelt: The Home Front in WWII* [1995]).

Chapter 19: Without Franklin

I interviewed David Roosevelt and Tommy's niece, Ellie Zartman. On Esther Lape's life after Eleanor, and on Eleanor's continued love for Franklin after his death, Joseph P. Lash's biography (*Eleanor and Franklin* [1971]) was a valued source. Regarding the fate of the Village and Robert Moses's attempted transformation of the area, I relied on John Strausbaugh's *The Village: 400 Years of Beats and Bohemians, Radicals and Rogues: A History of Greenwich Village* (2014).

Chapter 20: Eleanor and John F. Kennedy

Eleanor continued to be politically influential throughout the 1950s and until her death, supporting Adlai Stevenson and JFK's presidential runs, as documented by Allida M. Black in *Casting Her Own Shadow: Eleanor Roosevelt and the Shaping of*

Postwar Liberalism (1996) and Hazel Rowley in *Franklin and Eleanor: An Extraordinary Marriage* (2011).

Chapter 21: The First Feminist

On Eleanor's friendship and travels with Dr. David Gurewitsch, I've depended on his wife Edna's book, *Kindred Souls* (Edna P. Gurewitsch, *Kindred Souls: The Friendship of Eleanor Roosevelt and David Gurewitsch* [2002]). Eleanor was not pleased with David's marriage to Edna, as Edna recounts. Eleanor's appearance alongside Frank Sinatra on television can be found on YouTube. *The New York Times* has reported extensively on the social changes to the Village over the past seven decades.

Index

Key to abbreviations:
FDR = Franklin Delano Roosevelt
JFK = John F. Kennedy
TR = Theodore Roosevelt

INDEX

INDEX

INDEX

Hyde Park, N.Y., Roosevelt estate
   (Springwood), 17, 40, 108, 113
   children sent to, World War I,
      63, 64
   Eleanor's funeral and, 191
   Eleanor's wedding night at, 50–51
   FDR and Eleanor buried at, 191
   FDR's affair and, 65
   FDR's childhood at, 40–41
   FDR's recovery from polio and, 96
   Franklin D. Roosevelt Presidential
      Library and Museum at, 15,
      181
   Roosevelt family caretaker, 50

Imitation of Life (Hurst), 122

Jackson, Robert Houghwout, 163
Jacobs, Jane, 182
James, Henry, 32
Johnson, Lady Bird, 133
Johnson, Lyndon B., 184
Jones, LeRoy, 96, 100
Josephson, Barney, 111
Jung, Carl, 74
   "the participation mystique,"
      28–29

Kafka Was the Rage (Broyard), 170
Kennedy, John F., 153, 183, 184–86,
   189, 191
Kennedy, Joseph P., 185
Kindred Souls (Gurewitsch), 187

La bohème (Puccini), 72
Ladies' Home Journal, 110
Lape, Esther Everett, 80, 82, 178,
   181, 204n
   American Peace Award
      Committee and, 110
   Eleanor and, 80, 81, 100, 101,
      140

FBI file on, 109
home on East 11th St., 81, 82,
   147
relationship with Elizabeth Read,
   80, 86
New Woman Movement and,
   80, 81
See also Read, Elizabeth
Larooco houseboat, 100–101
Lash, Jonathan, 156, 161
Lash, Joseph, 15, 155–62
   on Eleanor and Earl Miller, 132
   Eleanor and Franklin, 90
   on Eleanor and public office, 181
   on Eleanor at *Grief* statue, 69
   at Eleanor's apartment, 158
   Eleanor's books and, 160–61
   on Eleanor's love for FDR, 179
   government surveillance of,
      159–60
   in Greenwich Village, 161
   HUAC hearings and, 155–56,
      203n
   at Hyde Park and Val-Kill,
      158–59
   interviews with child psychiatrist
      Bernard, about Eleanor, 15
   meets Eleanor, 155
   Publishers Weekly interview,
      160–61
   radical leftwing politics of,
      155–57
   stationed at Chanute Field,
      159–60
   Trude Pratt and, 159, 160
Lash, Trude Pratt, 159, 160,
   187–89
Last Call (Okrent), 77
La vie de bohème (Murger), 72
League of Nations, 84, 109
League of Women Voters, 80, 84,
   107, 200n

INDEX

Eleanor's debut in, 37–38

Eleanor's final years, East 74th St., 189–90

Eleanor teaching immigrant girls, 43–44

electric streetlights introduced, 2

FDR Drive, 141

FDR-Eleanor's wedding, 47–50

first buildings with electricity, 11

first railroad, 11

first telephones, 11

"The Four Hundred," 3, 4

Grand Central Terminal, 122

Great Depression and, 148

growth of, 10–11

Hall family brownstone, 37th St., 27

immigrants in, 2, 11–12

Knickerbocker Bowling Club, 7

Knickerbocker Club, 24

Metropolitan Telephone and Telegraph Company, 11

Moses and urban renewal, 181–82

Neighborhood Playhouse, 120

Prohibition and, 76, 77

Roosevelt residence, East 65th St., 53, 64, 94, 141

St. Patrick's Day Parade, 48

subway lines, 73

tenements and slums, 11, 44, 120

TR as head of Police Department, 12

TR's bike squad, 12

Vanderbilt costume ball, 1–7, 197n

Vanderbilt mansion, 1, 4, 5

wealthiest citizens, neighborhoods, 2

World War II and, 169–70

See also Greenwich Village

New York Consumers' League, 121

New York Herald, 23

New York Herald Tribune, 147

New York State

  Bureau of Women in Industry, 129

  Democratic Party in, 85, 121, 125

  Eleanor as First Lady of, 123–25

  Eleanor as political leader, 181

  Eleanor campaigning for Al Smith for governor, 106–7

  Eleanor's inspection tours, 130

  FDR as governor, 122, 123–33, 182

  FDR as state senator, 57–58, 89

  Perkins as labor commissioner, 128–29

  TR as governor, 126

  TR as state assemblyman, 11–12

  Women's Division of the Democratic Committee, 106

New York Times

  American Peace Award Committee report, 110

  Eleanor as First Lady of Albany, 123

  Eleanor-FDR wedding, 49–50

  on Eleanor organizing women to vote, 105

  electrification of *Times* building, 11

  report on FDR's polio, 93

  on Val-Kill furniture, 118

  on Vanderbilt's costume ball, 5

New York World, 92

Nin, Anaïs, 73

Nixon, Richard, 184

No Ordinary Time (Goodwin), 67, 174

Obama, Michelle, 190

O'Day, Caroline, 117

Okrent, Daniel, *Last Call*, 77

Olivia (Bussy), 33–34

Oyster Bay, N.Y., 9, 10, 20

213

INDEX

INDEX

Roosevelt, Eleanor, politics and as
    activist, Democratic party (*cont.*)
  as FDR's "eyes and legs," 107–8,
    130
  FDR's nominating speech for Al
    Smith and, 102–4
  as FDR's policy adviser, 44, 172
  as FDR's political partner, 59, 61,
    66, 67, 90, 94, 96, 99, 104–5,
    107–8, 125–26, 130, 133, 138,
    141, 200n
  FDR's support for women's
    suffrage and, 59
  fund-raising by, 63
  having to "think like men" and,
    105
  Howe meetings and, 128
  JFK and, 184–86, 189, 204n
  loyalty to FDR, 138
  organizing women to vote, 105
  progressive social programs and,
    126, 129, 131, 138, 172
  as public speaker, 85, 107
  radio addresses, 107
  speaking for women's
    organizations, 106
  Stevenson and, 183, 184, 204n
Roosevelt, Eleanor, presidency of
    FDR
  in Appalachia, New Deal for
    miners and Arthurdale project,
    150–51, 203n
  Christmas at the White House,
    151
  effort to end lynching laws, 152–53
  FDR's death and notifying
    Truman, 170–71
  FDR wins 1932 election, 138
  fears of losing independence,
    146–47
  as First Lady, 141–42, 145–54,
    169, 179–80, 202–3n

  Hickok at the White House, 138,
    141
  HUAC hearings and, 157, 203n
  Inauguration Day and, 146, 147
  media keeps her secrets and, 147
  private secretary, Tommy
    Thompson, and, 160
  refusal to live full-time at the
    White House, 147
  resignation from the DAR over
    Anderson discrimination, 153
  staying in Greenwich Village, 152,
    158
  White House press conferences
    for women journalists started
    by, 138
  World War II and, 180
Roosevelt, Eleanor, quotations
  on being heroes, 44
  on building character, 187
  on campaign behavior for wives,
    145
  on doing what is right, 135
  on dreams and the future, 37
  on forgiveness, 68
  on great minds, 123
  on hope, 190
  on importance of curiosity, 9
  on learning a "liberating thing,"
    61
  on looking fear in the face, 57
  on love, 27, 79
  on meeting whatever comes, 177
  message to her students, 119–20
  "No one can make you feel
    inferior," 109
  on the obligation to be an
    individual, 163
  on shaping our lives, 19
  on Val-Kill, 113
  on what you need to be doing, 71
  on the White House years, 169

218

INDEX

INDEX

About the Author

Jan Jarboe Russell is the author of the *New York Times* bestseller *The Train to Crystal City: FDR's Secret Prisoner Exchange Program and America's Only Family Internment Camp During World War II*, winner of the Texas Institute of Letters Prize for Best Book of Nonfiction. She is a Neiman Fellow, a contributing editor for *Texas Monthly*, and has written for the *San Antonio Express-News*, *The New York Times*, *Slate*, and other magazines. She also compiled and edited *They Lived to Tell the Tale: True Stories of Modern Adventure from the Legendary Explorers Club*. She lives in San Antonio, Texas, with her husband, Dr. Lewis F. Russell Jr.